Of Life and Horses

Cooperation Through Communication

Ann Nyberg Bradley

Cover artwork by Debby Smith

Copyright © 2011 Ann Nyberg Bradley
All rights reserved.

ISBN: 1-4611-3243-6
ISBN-13: 9781461132431

Dedication

*I dedicated my first book to the past—my parents.
I'd like to dedicate this book to the future—my daughter Lisa Tolin McNelly
and my grandson Jamie.
You are my inspiration in life.
My hope is that Jamie will grow up to value
nature and wildlife and live his life in harmony with
all Mother Nature has bestowed upon us.
The future lies with you.*

Table of Contents

- Introduction — xi
- The Language of Communication — 1
- Underlying Intentions & Expectations — 15
  1. Feel — 23
  2. Drive/Draw — 24
  3. The Bear — 25
  4. The Pendulum Swing — 27
- Dominance & Submission — 31
- The Flip Side of the Coin — 37
- Point of View — 41
- Punishment vs. Reward — 43
- First Impulse — 55
- Power Over Fear — 61
- Anxiety/Tension and Release — 67
- Mind to Feet Connection — 73
- The Rein Aids — 79
- Primary & Secondary Aids — 87
- Balance vs. Counter-balance — 93
- Resistance and Evasion — 97
- Persistence vs. Insistence — 103
- The Wind Sock — 107
- In the Middle — 111
- Summary — 115

The Legend of the Spirit Horse

Many Indian tribes would kill the horses
of braves slain in battle
so they would not be separated
in the next world.
This was considered the highest honor
to the brave and his horse.
Spirit horses were not bound to earth
so they had no hooves.
They glided on exaggerated hair in their
mane, tail and legs.

-Debby Smith, artist

Acknowledgements

I'd like to thank Alison Nordholm for her feedback and editing tips, although this book has been sitting on my computer for 6 years so she may not even remember doing so.

Thank you to Terie Zimmerman for her more recent and excellent advice on ways to make the material more readable.

And last but not least, thank you to Nancy Horne for doing the graphic design work on the cover. You took my vision and made it a reality.

Introduction

The prevalent theme of this book is communication which implies understanding. Ultimately the human/horse union is one in which our mind controls the horse's body. We supply the brains and the horse supplies the brawn, so to speak, and we want to create a synergistic union which utilizes those strengths to an advantage neither of us could achieve without the other. The way to achieve this is through the horse's understanding of what we want. Some riders will attempt to physically control a horse's body, but he knows how to operate his body far better and more effectively than we do. So in that sense, if we can convey the idea of what we want then we can let him do it. In that manner our aids can remain light, polite, and tactful. The first step in gaining a horse's understanding is in realizing that is our aim. There are some riders who seem to think their role is to physically manipulate a horse through the use of rough aids and/or the infliction of pain, and those riders will need to first realize it is the mind to mind communication that is lacking in their riding.

There are different ways to achieve understanding, and one effective method is clicker training. [1] I find it works well with horses, and more importantly it works well with people. Understanding can occur in the horse as a light bulb moment. It can occur in one instant when he suddenly realizes *"Hey, you aren't just trying to annoy, scare, or hurt me—you're trying to tell me something"*. I've seen that moment occur in many horses and you can see the wheels turning in their heads as they figure it out. My favorite analogy is related to Helen Keller. There was a movie made in 1962 starring Patty Duke as Helen and Anne Bancroft as her teacher. Helen was blind, deaf and mute and her parents wanted Annie to only teach her the skills to get along in life—like sitting down at the dinner table, eating with utensils, etc. But Annie wanted more. Annie wanted Helen to understand. Annie wanted Helen to be able to communicate, so she persisted in teaching her sign language. Helen learned to mimic the signs, and she learned to make the associations between the signs and objects, but then in a tear-jerking scene at the end of the movie she realized that the purpose of the sign language was communication. She **understood**. I have come to call that moment of understanding with horses a *Helen Keller moment*, yet I mean no disrespect at all. Helen Keller was an idol of mine when I was young, and I greatly admire her achievements.

That moment of understanding is just as fulfilling and inspirational when it occurs with a horse as it was in the movie. It is literally the meeting of two minds, and when it occurs it changes the relationship and the interaction between the two parties. It does carry with it a responsibility on our part to continue an interactive relationship based in communication and not revert back to cruder ways of gaining performance, but if we will make that commitment it is very much worthwhile. When we gain a horse's cooperation through communication we have more than an animal at our disposal—we have a special bond with another living being. A bond like no other.

- Ann Bradley

The Language of Communication

Our training goal with our horses should not be blind obedience obtained by any means, but rather *cooperation through communication*. We want to elicit in the horse a willingness to carry out our desires, and the first step in that endeavor is to develop a common language between us. The language needs to be developed when we are both calm and attentive to one another because defensiveness in either party interferes with communication. Since we are the instigators of the human/horse relationship, it is up to us to learn to interact with a language the horse will understand. Many of the problems I see humans experience with horses are directly related to a lack of communication which leads to confusion.

To communicate effectively we need to develop a language via our bodies and our actions that will express to the horse our wishes—i.e. an effective body language. We can communicate through actions that the horse visibly sees, like in groundwork where we are a visual entity—or we can communicate through an actual physical feel, like the aids given by our body when on the horse's back. Either way, the language needs to be one that makes sense to him. It doesn't matter how correct we think we are, if the horse doesn't understand then the language is ineffective. So how do we know if he understands? The answer is in his response. If I say to you *"Please have a seat"*, and you say *"Yes, the weather is lovely"*, then I know you either didn't hear me or you didn't understand what I said. But if you say *"Thank you, I will"*, then I know you heard and understood. In that sense, a correct response from a horse is a good indicator that he understood the request.

There are two sides to the communication issue—*speaking* and *listening*. What we convey through body language to a horse is important, and is a language we'll need to spend some time learning, but the ingredient I see lacking too often is the other half of the communication equation—i.e. listening. Whether we're communicating with a horse or another person, how do we know what to say if we don't listen? We listen to a horse by observing how he responds to what we do. It is by gauging his responses to our actions that determines whether or not he understood what we said. If we do something and he responds as we wanted, then either he understood or he got lucky and did the right thing anyway. Even if he got lucky, we should reward his correct response and then ask him again. If he'll give the right answer three times in a row, then we can rest assured he very likely understood the question and knows the answer. So it is through observing the horse's responses that we know how to respond back to him.

When the human is unable to communicate his desires to the horse in a way the horse can understand, and when the horse doesn't respond as desired, the human often assumes the horse is being obstinate or defiant and they *scream* at him. I don't mean literally scream (though I have seen that on occasion), but rather they scream through their body language and/or actions. Hitting, whipping, spurring, yanking, jerking, or throwing the upper body around when riding are all ways humans scream at horses. And many times the only reason the horse didn't do what the human wanted was because he didn't understand. The human failed in his efforts to communicate. *Screaming* at a horse is just as futile as, say, going to Italy and screaming at the Italians in English because they don't do as we say. If we go to Italy and they only speak Italian, then we need to learn to speak Italian. Speaking the language doesn't give us a 100% guarantee the person we are speaking to will comply with our request, but at least they will understand it. Yet if they don't even understand our request, their non-compliance is almost guaranteed.

The concept of empathy opens the door to the understanding and acceptance of a differing viewpoint and motivation, and horses and humans certainly have different perspectives in life. To empathize with another does not mean we have to adopt their viewpoint in life, but it involves an attempt to at least understand their perspective. It is our responsibility to understand the horse, not the other way around. We are supposed to be the more intelligent species, plus we are the ones who have dictated that horses live in our world—they had no say in that matter. It is our responsibility on many levels—physically, intellectually, emotionally and spiritually—to understand and accommodate the nature of these animals we have chosen to govern and use to our own purpose. A little empathy goes a long way.

When training a horse, there is a distinction between obedience and willing cooperation. It is possible to obtain obedience and/or submission through force, fear, pain, and/or intimidation, but willing cooperation can only be offered by the horse. You can't *make* a horse be willingly cooperative, you can only encourage his willing cooperation by creating in him trust, confidence and desire combined with education. There is also a distinction between blind obedience and trust. Some riders think if a horse will blindly do whatever they request, it must be out of trust. Blind obedience can be a component of trust, but trust is not necessarily a component of blind obedience. Sometimes a horse is blindly obedient because he's afraid to be otherwise, and that is not the same thing as doing something out of trust and willingness.

The difference between blind obedience born out of intimidation and willing cooperation is the horse's underlying state of being. A horse can obediently do as we request and still be afraid, confused and/or anxious in the process. A horse who is willingly cooperative will be calm, trusting and confident as his underlying state of being. The differences between the two states can be seen in his general demeanor as displayed by his eyes, ears, tail, body language, and the way he moves his feet. The bottom line is we want to address a horse's underlying state of being in our interaction with him and make sure he's *alright* inside as the foundation or basis for our training.

Some people think things like trust, confidence, calmness, and willingness are merely touchy-feely qualities—i.e. they are nice, but they don't see the relevance to equine performance. There are numerous reasons to instill those qualities in our horses, such as an enhanced relationship, quality interaction, and the overall well-being of the horse, but one compelling reason is that those qualities make horses safer for us to be around. So even if someone has no desire to develop a truly harmonious partnership with a horse, they should at least be interested in getting him *alright* inside if for no other reason than their own safety. Behaviors reflect the inner state of being, and the behaviors that arise from a state of inner turmoil can be dangerous.

Horses communicate with one another and with us through their body language, and all those behaviors they exhibit that we don't like, such as bucking, rearing, bolting, biting, kicking, and striking, are a horse's way of *screaming* at us. A horse that routinely exhibits any of these behaviors is desperate to be heard. The only way he has to tell us something is wrong is to display it through his actions, so while we don't like those actions, we still need to realize they are his way of telling us something is wrong. He is likely either confused, in pain or discomfort, distracted, afraid, frustrated, resentful, etc. Whatever the reason, the answer is not to punish his actions but to figure out how to rectify the underlying state of being so he doesn't need to behave that way. The behaviors are merely his means of communication. How else can he communicate to us what he is feeling?

Often times horses will communicate those feelings to us in more subtle ways at first, and if we ignore those initial attempts at communication then he will *raise his voice*. The more subtle means of communication include movements he makes with his ears, eyes, tail, and posture or stance. He will raise his voice by using his teeth, feet, and body. We need to learn to listen more closely to him while he's still speaking in a lower voice, before he feels he has to scream.

I know some people who think horses have no right to hold their own ideas or opinions, and I can only say I feel very sorry for their animals. What a miserable life it would be for any living being to know you are never heard. I have found with many horses that simply showing them we hear and acknowledge what they have to say is enough to elicit their compliance to our request. Other times, what they have to say will determine our approach. I'll use a child as an example, because the situation is easier to understand, but the

Of Life and Horses

underlying philosophy is the same with horses. Say you ask your 10 year old to take his dirty dishes into the kitchen after dinner, and he says, or implies, *"No"*. Let's say you're also a conscientious parent and you want to handle situations like this in the best possible manner, so you ask him why he's unwilling. He gives you 1 of the following 4 answers:

1. *Because I'm afraid to go into the kitchen. It's dark in there and I'm afraid there's a boogey-man hiding behind the door.*
2. *I WILL take my dishes into the kitchen, but this TV show is almost over and I'd really like to see the ending. Can't I do it in a few minutes when the show is over?*
3. *I twisted my ankle playing soccer this afternoon and it really hurts when I walk on it. Could you take my dishes into the kitchen tonight?*
4. *Because I don't want to and you can't make me, you old bag!*

If you look at this situation written out like this, it's pretty obvious to see that each answer should be dealt with differently. In the case of answer #1, the parent could go into the kitchen with the child and show him how to turn on the light before he enters, then show him there are no boogey-men hiding in there. Answer #2 is a reasonable request—why not cut him some slack and let him watch the rest of his TV show? Answer #3 is also valid, and something that needs to be dealt with—perhaps a trip to the doctor is in order. Yet how many people (especially when dealing with horses) automatically assume that the reason for any non-compliance is #4? They automatically assume that any *"No"* is absolute defiance and rebellion, when actually that is very seldom the case. And when it is the case, it isn't something that happened suddenly. It has likely been coming on for some time. In addition to which, if the response you receive is #4, then taking the dinner dishes to the kitchen is beside the point. The dishes may be the battleground, but they are not the issue. If the answer you receive is #4, forget the dishes, there are far more pervasive and serious fundamental issues in the relationship to deal with than taking the dishes to the kitchen.

I see this same type of scenario played out with horses and humans as well; for example, a horse hesitates in crossing a creek because he's unsure of the footing and his rider assumes he's being openly defiant; or a horse pulls his head up when being bridled because the human clangs the metal bit on his teeth when inserting it in his mouth, and the human thinks the horse is being insubordinate; or the horse has no ground manners because he's full of anxiety and tension and just wants out of there, but the human thinks he's being rude or willful, etc. Horses do what we consider to be *bad* things for a reason, and the reason is least often pure defiance—at least initially. Horses, however, can learn that the best defense is a good offense, but in those cases, the horse learned to be defiant. When that happens it's a case of the behavior began for one reason but continued for another.

When horses don't comply with a request, I find the most common reasons are one or more of the following:

- Confusion
- Fear
- Pain/Discomfort
- Lack of Confidence
- Distraction
- Management Issues
- Agenda

1. Confusion exists due to a lack of understanding and the horse doesn't know what it is we want. Unlike with the child, we don't share a common verbal language with horses, and that's where the miscommunication occurs. Consistent confusion very often leads to frustration and/or resentment, especially if the horse is punished for his lack of understanding. This is probably the most common reason for non-compliance in a horse, though it runs a close race with the next most common reason:
2. Fear can range from mild apprehension to outright panic. If the fear is at the lower end of the scale, such as mild

apprehension or wariness, it can lead to a hesitation, while panic can lead to an outright refusal or an attempt to actually escape the situation. But fear, no matter the degree, is not defiance! Fear needs to be worked through, and if the non-compliance is fear-based, then working through the fear will lead to compliance.

3. Pain/Discomfort or the anticipation of pain—Just like the child who sprained his ankle, horses experience a myriad of pains often due to the physical exertions we place on them. Pain is a valid reason for non-compliance. Though it's not always easy to diagnose, it is a good thing to rule out pain when faced with chronic training problems. When I used to gallop racehorses back in the 1980's I used as my basic gauge of the workload *ankles & attitude*, meaning I checked ankles every day for any heat, swelling or fill, and I looked for any deterioration in attitude, no matter how slight (such as a brief pinning of the ears when approached with the saddle, or a swish of the tail). A change in attitude for the worse is very often an early indicator of either pain or work overload. If I backed off the work load at the slightest sign of a problem I could usually get by with only a few days off. But many other trainers would chalk up attitude problems as defiance and push the horse to work anyway. They often ended up with more serious injuries requiring a lay-up of weeks or months. Back pain is rather common in horses, and it often leads to undesired behavior and/or a bad attitude. If a horse is acting out under saddle it would be prudent to rule out back pain which can be caused by an ill-fitting saddle, poor riding, a horse not conditioned to do the work being asked for, imbalanced feet, tension or anxiety in the performance, sore hocks/stifles, etc. Not all pain results in limping, and often times the pain that leads to behavioral problems does not manifest as a limp.

4. Lack of Confidence—When we are riding a horse we are essentially asking him to *go first*. The leader to a horse is a visual entity, and we are visual to a horse when we are on the ground but not when on his back, unless he turns his head—and even if he sees us back there, in his mind

he is still going first. That's not such an issue with horses who naturally possess leadership qualities, but it can be a real challenge for horses who are confirmed followers. A lack of confidence can cause a horse to balk. Horses who are confirmed followers don't make the best candidates for sports requiring them to be leaders or to be bold in their performances. Some people notice the horse in a herd who stands back and appears timid and they like him because he seems sweet and demure, and maybe he is, but horses who are timid possess just as many training challenges as horses who are dominant. The timid horse requires a confident human leader.

Another contributing factor I have noticed is that we expect horses to progress in their performance much faster than we did 40 or 50 years ago. When I started riding we used to allow horses a chance to plateau in their performance progression, and it was during those plateau periods when their confidence level could rise up to their performance level. But we are in such a hurry nowadays that we never give horses that chance to feel competent and confident in their work before we're already asking them to do more. We end up with a big gap between performance requests and their level of confidence. A horse who is 7 to 9 years of age is one who is just entering his adult prime, yet how many horses of that age do we see who are already used up, sour, or lame?

5. Distraction—This is similar to the child who wasn't really refusing to take his dishes into the kitchen, rather he wanted to finish his TV show first. Distraction is something to play by ear. It can be a mild form of fear, which means if you don't allow the horse to work through the distraction, it could escalate into fear. But it can also be simply distraction, as in *"I'd RATHER look at those horses over there right now".* I don't punish distraction regardless of the cause, but I do continue to bring the horse's attention back to me and/or the job at hand until he's able or willing to focus on it. Occasionally I'll ride a horse who has learned to use distraction to avoid work. This is where the issue of distraction can be tricky because it's

a judgment call whether the cause of the distraction is fear or simple inattentiveness. If I suspect it's a learned evasion I don't punish him for it, but I'll take away the payoff by increasing the work request, and then easing off when I feel his attention come back to me. In that way he's rewarded for paying attention and he works harder when distracted.

6. <u>Management issues</u> can play a role in training problems. Horses who are overfed and/or under exercised can be too fresh or full of themselves to optimally benefit from their training lessons. Freshness can also cause horses to exaggerate whatever behaviors they already have a tendency to display. For example, a mildly spooky horse might spook at everything in sight when he's fresh; or a horse who frequently humps up his back when he canters could give some outright bucks when he's fresh; or the horse who is usually strong in the bridle could run off when he has too much pent up energy. Horses need adequate turn out time, and they need enough room to run and buck and play at liberty. The more they are able to move, the better. Their whole systems (structural, mental/emotional, respiratory, and digestive) are designed for access to low impact, continual movement. Simply turning a stabled horse out in the arena and letting him run and/or buck before you ride him can, in some cases, make a huge difference in how well he rides and how much attention he pays to you. It seems many of the chronic joint problems we see in horses today are in some part related to their overall lack of ability to move around at will. We keep them confined to stalls, then ride them (often too hard) in a short, concentrated sessions, then put them back into a confined area where they basically stand. That type of regime goes against their nature and design. It's a well known fact that the ability to move freely is beneficial for many arthritic conditions as well as their frame of mind.

7. <u>Agenda</u> is another reason a horse will not comply to a request, meaning he has his own ideas about what is worthy of his attention and effort. Mares frequently have

their own agendas in life and they get a bad rap for it. In the wild the lead mare is the one who makes all the little daily decisions, like when to go to water, where to graze, when to hang out under the shade tree, etc. Stallions have basically 3 agendas: get mares, keep mares, and breed mares—and although a stallion's agendas are very strong, they are usually limited to those 3 areas in his life. That means that if his herd is safe, his mares are bred, and no other stallions are threatening him then he's usually happy to follow the daily routine of the lead mare. That's why geldings are so popular as riding horses—i.e. when we take away their agendas as stallions they are usually pretty compliant. Mares, on the other hand, can be considered the micro-managers of herd life, and in domestic situations that can translate to mean they can remember exactly how many circles you did yesterday and in which direction and will question why you dare to change that routine today. Obviously not all mares, stallions and geldings fit this profile, but overall it holds some truth; and, if nothing else, it reminds us that horses are individuals with differing outlooks in life.

In some cases, the reason a horse *says no* is due to actual defiance, though more often it can be due to a lack of respect. Some people think a lack of respect is the same thing as defiance, but for a horse, a lack of respect is related to a lack of leadership—in other words, it's an unresolved issue of hierarchy. A horse wants to know that *someone* is in charge, and if it's not the human, then he'll take over. So if he doesn't respect your position in the hierarchy, he may try to put himself above you. I see a distinction between the two. When I run into non-compliance I run through the list of possible reasons, and I put absolute defiance at the bottom of the list. I'll rule out the other possible reasons first, and most of the time there is another reason. I've ridden or handled over a thousand horses over the span of 50 plus years, and relatively few of those horses were truly defiant—and in some cases the ones that were had learned to be that way. Yet when I talk to other riders, the most common reason they give for their horse's problems are defiance, stubbornness, and/or willfulness.

Of Life and Horses

Horses can be loosely categorized as being *fear-oriented* or *agenda-oriented*, and not all domestic breeds of horses have the same fear factor that Nature instilled in the horse to insure his survival. If we pressure a fear-oriented horse we will trigger a fear reaction, but if we pressure an agenda-oriented horse we will more likely trigger frustration or resentment. The latter can lead to dangerous behavior. A fearful horse can certainly be dangerous, but he is acting defensively. His primary goal is his own safety. A resentful horse can act offensively, and he can intentionally try to inflict damage. If we punish a horse, we will likely trigger fear in the fear-oriented horse, but punishment is apt to trigger resentment in the agenda-oriented horse. The best way to deal with agenda is to figure out a way to remove the pay-off rather than punish the horse.

I remember an agenda-oriented horse I rode a number of years ago that had learned his owner wouldn't hold him to task if he threatened retaliation. If she rode him outside and he decided he wasn't in the mood to go over a creek or through mud she would let him turn around and go back to the barn. She asked me to ride him, and I decided to address his creek-crossing issue out on the trails. We came to a small ditch with a trickle of water in it, and he stopped dead in his tracks. He started to flip his head and I got the sense that if he could talk he would have said *"This is far enough. I want to go back to the barn now."* I could tell he wasn't afraid of the water or the footing—he just wasn't in the mood to continue. He had learned that balking held a payoff—i.e. going back to the barn.

I didn't want to fight with him and I didn't want to punish him, but I also wanted him to cross the ditch, so I devised a way to take away his pay-off for not crossing. He was at the edge of the ditch and clearly didn't want to go across, so I just kept him standing there facing the ditch. His first attempt to go back to the barn was to try to wheel around 180 degrees to the left, but I caught him before he had wheeled 90 degrees and used the right rein to bring him back so he was facing the ditch again. He stood there for a few minutes seemingly perplexed that this normally successful tactic hadn't worked. Then he tried to wheel around again and he was much quicker at it. I didn't get the wheel stopped before he'd gotten past the 90 degree point so I used the left rein to turn the wheel into a 360 degree turn which put him full circle and right back facing the ditch. At that point he became very frustrated. His next trick was to drop his head and try to buck, but as his feet came off the ground I booted him to go forward causing him to quickly back up as that was not the result he wanted. Finally his last resort was to fling his head around and attempt to bite my leg. The toe of my boot just happened to bump him in the mouth (accidentally on purpose), and he abandoned that tactic. At that point he just stood there weighing his options. He finally let out a big sigh and walked across the ditch. I praised him as we left the ditch behind and continued on through the woods and then back to the barn.

The next time I rode him we headed back out to the ditch. He hesitated for a moment or two and I just sat there keeping him facing the ditch. I figured if he tried anything it would be his signature wheel to the left, so I had my right rein ready to bring him back. He stood there poised to wheel and I sat there poised to bring him back, and all the while I could see the wheels turning in his head. He never did try to wheel and after a few minutes he let out a sigh and walked over the ditch. He never balked with me again. Had I fought with him or punished him for refusing to go over the ditch I would likely have triggered resentment, but as it was I merely took away his pay-off for not crossing. Agenda-oriented horses are often smart and they are *thinkers*. Our best plan of action with them is to try to set up a situation where they think their own way to our desired conclusion.

Another aspect of defiance is what I think of as the *mirror factor*. If we defy a horse we will set ourselves up to receive defiance in return. He will mirror back to us whatever it is we present to him. I find that to be a common cause of what many people consider to be defiance in horses. I think many people would be much better horse trainers if their horses were literal, rather than figurative, mirrors. That way people could visually see exactly what it is they are presenting to the horse—i.e. the way the horse sees them—because whatever we present, the horse will mirror back. If we present calmness, trust, respect, and confidence to a horse we greatly increase our chances of receiving calmness, trust, respect, and confidence back from him. So the next time you are not receiving back what you want to receive, *look in the mirror* to first see what it is you are presenting before you put all the blame on the horse.

Oprah Winfrey addressed this issue (though not relating to horses) in her online workshop: *Live Your Best Life*. In that workshop she said (essentially) that *"...cause is one with effect. If you participate in the cause, you can't help but create the effect."* She also said *"...intention forms thought; thought shapes action; and action creates consequence."* So when we perceive that a horse is being defiant, our underlying intention will automatically address defiance, and in that sense we become wrapped up in a battle of wills. The mere fact that we acknowledge it brings life to it—whatever *it* is. If we perceive our horse to be defiant, then we will automatically assume and present whatever posture, feeling and mindset we use when dealing with defiance, and by adopting that state of being, we give life or energy to the perception. In that way, we can cause defiance in a horse who was not being defiant to begin with! In that same way we can actually bring many things into our lives and they can be all the things we desperately do not want to experience. Our focus on what we don't want gives it life, which is why it is so important to keep our focus on the things we do want to happen and experience. That holds true whether one is dealing with horses or life in general. It's more of a life lesson, yet the repercussions are often instantaneous with a horse.

When we learn to listen to horses, we will see that the reason for non-compliance will be one of the above seven in the vast majority of cases. And none of those reasons warrant punishment! If we punish a horse's non-compliance for one of the above seven reasons, it is like saying to him *"Shut up! I don't care why you don't want to do this. I said do it, so you do it anyway."* Is that what you would say to the 10 year old child who's afraid to take his dishes into the dark kitchen? Yet that's what many horses *hear* in every encounter they have with human beings. Is it any wonder so many horses simply retreat within themselves, or become outwardly resentful toward humans or try to escape and be anyplace but where they are?

We can learn by watching masterful horsemen and women work with horses, but I think it is good to keep in mind the saying:

"Seek not to imitate the master; seek what the master sought." [2]

Many horse trainers will relay their own particular techniques in very exacting ways, indicating that you need to imitate their actions to a tee, but I disagree with this notion. I think everyone has their own style, their own feel, and their own expressions, and it's more important that you know clearly within yourself what it is you want to achieve vs. copying someone else's motions. If your intentions are clear enough and carry enough energy or life, they will come through in your actions.

I saw a well-known clinician one time who said you should never present your open hand to a horse because horses view that as predatory, like the open paw of a lion. And to validate his claim he then crouched down with his arms raised and his hands open with his fingers curled like claws, and sure enough the horse exhibited a fear reaction to him. However, in my own round pen or liberty work I routinely use a raised hand with an open palm as a *drawing signal*. I feel like I have a magnet in my palm and it's drawing the horse's energy and focus to me, and so far, I've never frightened a horse with my raised, open hand. I don't even know why I started using an open hand—I didn't learn it from someone else, it just sort of happened without my really thinking about it. It was my body's instinctive way of carrying out my mind's intention. But if I had vowed to never open my hand to a horse because someone else said not to, I would not have at my disposal what has turned out to be a very effective means of communication that works well for me. But there is more to this than meets the eye, which leads into the next chapter...

Underlying Intentions & Expectations

*The most important training tools we possess
are our underlying intentions and expectations.*

Our underlying intentions and expectations are projected through our body language. That is how we communicate with horses. I don't think this concept can be emphasized enough. It is the primary defining aspect of horsemanship, and due to its importance, it warrants considerable thought and understanding. When thinking of our intentions and expectations there are two criteria that need to be met:

1. <u>Our underlying intentions must take into account the well-being of the horse.</u> Our underlying intentions must first come from a pure heart, and then they must be specific. Intending to inflict pain or fear, or vent our own frustration or anger, or exert our own dominance in a manner devoid of empathy, or feed our own ego can all be very strong objectives, but they are not honorable. Based on what I see, most transgressions arise from either ignorance or ego. A typical example of the former was one student I remember who was working with her horse on the ground, and both were sort of floundering around, so I asked her exactly what it was she was trying to do, and she couldn't answer—she didn't know. Her demeanor was vague and she seemed to be thinking *"I don't know exactly what I'm after, but I'll know it when I see it."* We all find ourselves in that situation at times, but we need

to realize that mindset gives the horse no clear direction. Our horses in many ways are mind readers, but if it's confusion that exists in our mind, or a lack of clarity, that's what they will read. We need a clear understanding of what it is we're asking for in order to convey that request to the horse, and at the very least we need to never punish him for not responding lest the fault lie at our own feet. In addition...

2. <u>We must expect what we want.</u> This sounds blatantly obvious, yet I see riders all the time who routinely expect what they do not want. I know many times I have felt a horse tense up and think to myself *"Uh oh, he's probably going to _____<fill in the blank with buck, bolt, spook, spin, rear, etc.>"*? If our mind has ever wandered to any of the bad things that *could* happen, then we are unconsciously expecting what we do not want, and our body language will project that as an intention. This is the counter-productive aspect of thinking in the negative, or thinking in terms of what we don't want, because the *don't* part of it doesn't get translated. If we think *don't buck* the part that comes through as an intention is *buck* because by not wanting to experience a buck we resist what we expect will happen. Our body's resistance is felt by the horse which triggers his defensiveness—and the focus of the defensiveness in both parties is on *buck*. Our body language will project our negative thought/s and emotion/s to a horse, even if we think we're doing a good job of hiding them. One challenging lesson to learn is *the ability to be prepared for the worst while truly expecting the best.*

All good horse trainers have very clear underlying intentions—they know exactly what they want a horse to do—and they fully expect the horse to do it. The way they project those intentions can vary, which is why techniques can vary from one trainer to the next with consistent results. One trainer might stand this way and hold his hand that way, and another trainer will position himself differently, but they each know exactly what it is they want to accomplish, and it is those underlying intentions the horse can read like an open book.

Even if our intention is clear there can still be a little niggling doubt in the back of our mind that will sabotage our presentation. Some horses will fill in for us despite that doubt, but to other horses that doubt is just enough for them to feel a conflict in what we are presenting, and the conflict gives them an *out*—and some horses actually resent that conflicted feeling. We sometimes use anger to substitute for a clear intention or expectation, but if we are angry it is usually an attempt to cover up the feeling of uncertainty that what we are doing will actually work.

Technique is only as good as the conviction and clarity of the underlying intention that fuels it.

I remember a number of years ago I knew a woman who worked hard at learning to sit on her horse *just right,* and to give her aids in the correct manner, but she was very meek and passive inside. Her riding was technically correct, but there was no conviction to it—no life or energy. Her horse was lazy enough that he would rather ignore her requests than comply, so even getting him to trot was an effort for her. After a while, her husband decided the horse was expensive and he wanted to get his money's worth, so he began to ride the horse too. He didn't really care about being educated in his riding, he just wanted to get on the horse and ride. His method of asking the horse to trot was to curl his upper body forward, draw his heels upward as he clamped his whole leg on the horse's side, and then jiggle the reins at the horse as if to say *"Go on now".* His wife was much more sophisticated in her position and her aiding, and yet the horse was more responsive to her husband. The reason was because the husband, despite his unskilled and rudimentary techniques, had very clear underlying intentions and expectations. He knew exactly what he wanted that horse to do, and he fully expected the horse to comply, and the horse did. It was upsetting to the wife because she had spent much more time and effort learning to ride than her husband, but her intentions were almost completely lacking in conviction. It didn't matter how correct she was in the application of her aids, she had no conviction behind them, and the horse knew it.

Conviction is an energized thought. Thoughts can exist in our heads that contain no energy—they are just thoughts—but when we energize a thought it becomes a *feeling thought*. We not only think it in our heads, but we feel it in our gut and in our whole body. It is the life or energy behind our thoughts that our horses read, so if our thoughts have no life to them they have no meaning to the horse. I think of inner conviction being on a dial from low to high. If a horse is not paying attention the first thing I dial up is the energy of my intention. I dial that all the way up before I begin to dial up my physical aids. Horses soon learn to respond to the intention dial and the physical aids dials can remain low. It is the energy of an intention or expectation that creates body language—i.e. those subtle cues our bodies deliver seemingly of their own accord. If a thought never leaves the head the body language will be passive and contain no meaning for the horse. That's what was going on with this woman. Her husband's intentions and expectations contained great energy and they came out in his body language, even though his physical cues were uneducated. She may have had the same thoughts he did but there was no conviction to them.

Her husband is also a good example of the phenomenon known as *beginner's luck*. Such a thing does exist, and I believe it is due to the fact that the beginner, in his naiveté, has no idea of all the things that can go wrong; therefore, he fully expects everything to go right. The husband's aids were crude, rude and unrefined, but his underlying intentions and expectations were crystal clear. The true master exhibits refined and skillful techniques coupled with the conviction of clear intentions and expectations, but of those two ingredients, the conviction of one's intentions and expectations often supercedes skillful technique that lacks clarity or direction. The horse will be able to see through one's actions (or body language) to the intent that underlies them.

If the intent and the body language are one to the same purpose, the person will be speaking clearly to the horse.

Unfortunately there often exists a conflict between the two. A person can intellectually (or mentally) want a horse to do something, but emotionally he doesn't. For example, the fearful rider who wants to appear braver than he is might spur his horse vigorously to go faster, yet he pulls the reins inward (and adopts a fetal pose) as he does because emotionally he's afraid of the horse's potential power or speed. Those two aids are conflicting: the spurs say *go* while the reins say *don't go*, so in essence he applies an *emotional parking brake* as he steps on the gas, and the worst part of that situation is that the horse can't win! If he doesn't go, then he's opposing the person's mental desire, but if he does go, he's opposing the person's emotional insecurity. So he will likely get punished either way, whether intentionally or not, because his rider is conflicted between his own mental desire and his emotional uncertainty.

What's the answer? Does that mean that no one should ride a horse until or unless he's accomplished and experienced enough to be truly effective? No, it doesn't mean that at all. Most horses are extremely forgiving creatures. Many will gladly tolerate a rider's emotional insecurities and physical lack of skill as long as the rider doesn't punish or blame the horse for his own failings. Show your horse a little appreciation for his tolerance, thank him for being so forgiving, and most horses will willingly work with you as your riding skills improve.

I've experienced two situations over the years that really stand out in my mind regarding underlying intentions and expectations. The first occurred when I was a teen-ager. The owner of the stable where I rode would get in truckloads of horses, and all of us kids would pick out a couple horses to ride and work with. I was never aggressive enough to get the best horses, so I usually ended up riding the ones no one else wanted. One time I ended up with a young bay gelding who seemed nice enough, except as I was riding him I thought he must be rather stupid. He barely had any steering or brakes, and he was a challenge to ride, but I persisted for about 20 or 30 minutes doing the best I could, and he did get a little better.

About that time the stable owner came into the arena to watch the horses going and he saw me on this gelding at the far end of the arena. He yelled at me to *"Get off that horse! He's not broke yet."* To this day I can still recall my reaction. At first it was one of enlightenment, I thought to myself *"Aha! No wonder he doesn't know anything".* With that, I turned to walk him back to the exit gate to dismount, but as I did another thought entered my mind—i.e. that I had been riding an unbroken horse. At that point, for the first time during the entire ride, doubt entered my mind. My thoughts went from *"THIS is what I want and expect you to do"* to *"Hmmm...I wonder what you'll do now?"* I made no real overt physical change that I was aware of, yet my doubt alone was just enough to turn the tables. By thinking in my own mind *"I wonder what you'll do now?"* I essentially turned that decision over to the horse, and when that decision was left up to him, he decided to put his head between his knees and buck so hard he sent me into the rafters (well.. not literally). The only reason I had been able to ride him as well as I had that first 20 or 30 minutes was because there was NO doubt in my mind that I could! I assumed he was broke and that I could ride him, and I did so with complete conviction and confidence, and he did his best to live up to my expectations. But once I allowed doubt to enter my demeanor, he was able to get his metaphorical foot into the crack of that opening door, but I was the one who opened the door for him, even if all I did was open it a crack.

This example is a bit extreme, because insecure riders get along with uneducated horses all the time, though it's generally considered an unwise pairing. The reason this episode resulted in such an extreme reaction from that horse was because he had zero foundation of training to fall back on. The only reason he had performed at all was because I was 100% convinced he could, so as soon as my conviction waned, his lack of training became quite evident. I use this example to point out the significance of one's underlying intentions and expectations, however, this degree of certainty can be unreliable. It's often present in the rank beginner, like the husband who naively expected his horse to do exactly as he bid, but then the rider enters another phase, and that degree of certainty can wane.

The beginning rider often doesn't even know what can happen on a horse, but with more experience, he realizes that all sorts of bad things are possible, and that knowledge can erode his confidence.

This middle phase can take years to work through, until the rider comes out fully confident again, and this time, when he's *come through* to the other side, his confidence is based on experience and knowing there are reliable outcomes. So the skilled and confident horseman, the one who has complete faith in his underlying intentions and expectations, may have no more confidence than the raw beginner, but the difference is the skilled horseman's confidence is based on years of experience with reliable results while the beginner's confidence is based on naiveté. In between those two extremes are a whole bunch of riders who might be thinking *"I was a better rider when I didn't know anything than I am now!"* I know that thought well. Been there/done that, as they say.

Then there is another category of confident riders—they are the ones who have more guts than sense. I was one of those riders too as a teen-ager. If those riders can accumulate the necessary experience without getting hurt and/or scared in the process, they can become fully confident without going through that middle phase of insecurity and doubt. But sometimes they are the ones you watch and can only shake your head knowing that God looks after those that need it most. I've seen people do really careless and foolish things around horses. I've done many stupid things myself, with no ill effects, but that's luck not skill.

The second example of the power of underlying expectation involved a young Thoroughbred mare my husband bought off a racetrack in California and hauled back to our farm. She'd had a long trailer ride, so after she'd had some time to settle in, I tied her up to a tree to give her a bath. I had been bathing her and hosing her off for a good 20 minutes when my husband came out and said *"Don't tie that mare up! She doesn't tie."* My first thought was *"She doesn't??"*, because I'd had her tied for over 20 minutes and she'd been fine. But at that point I took a step back away from her and my mindset changed from being completely absorbed in the act of bathing her to looking to see if she *might* pull back on the tie. And with that she immediately set back against the rope and pulled and shook her head and neck so violently I thought she might break her neck if the rope didn't break first. As with the unbroken colt, the only thing that changed was that doubt entered my mind and my demeanor. I lost my focus and I *turned the situation over to the horse,* and that was all she needed.

Suffice it to say, the conviction of our underlying intentions and expectations are the things our horses will read in our body language. There is no fooling the horse! However, not all horses will react negatively to what they read either. My examples were extreme. Some people may think they are fooling their horse because he does what they want him to do, but the horse who has a big heart and a generous nature may try his hardest to do the right thing despite the lack of confidence or direction the human gives him. Or another horse may do the right thing because what he sees in the human scares him. In that sense, he does the *right* thing because he's afraid to do the *wrong* thing, and not because he feels empathy, patience, respect, and clarity in the human's intentions. But there are many horses who do the right things for the wrong reasons which can fool some people into thinking they are doing the right thing in their training!

If you have any doubt, ask yourself first if your heart is pure and if you approach a horse from a place of love. Just for the record, I define love as the unconditional acceptance of another being for who and what they are, so when I say to approach a horse with love, I mean to accept him just as he is, with no judgment or criticism or blame. Pure love does not come from ego. I refer to love in the universal sense, and not in the myriad of ways humans can use the term—i.e. ways that relate to and/or feed the ego. So in that context, what *feeling* emanates from your being when you approach a horse? What *feeling* do you bring to the table?? Is it anger or frustration or fear or confusion or criticism or insecurity? Or is it love and acceptance and consideration and respect and confidence? When you ask your horse to do something, do you have an inner feeling of being his cheerleader? Do you silently desire and encourage him to get it right? Or do you look for all the little things he does wrong that you can criticize or punish? Whatever feeling we present will be the feeling he mirrors back to us. Sometimes he'll mirror back through opposition, other times he'll mirror back by trying to leave our presence entirely, or by trying to *make himself small* (by emotionally hiding). Some people think the latter reaction is a good thing, but I don't see it that way.

Any of those reactions is a sign that the horse is not *alright* inside. And even when we offer him the *good deal*, if he's been treated badly in the past he may not change instantly. It can be a process and will take some time to show him that his interactions with humans are different now than they used to be.

- **Feel**

Feel is the foundation of training. Feel can be a physical hands-on sensation or it can be palpable though not physical. For example, you can feel when someone is angry even if they don't lay a hand on you. Their anger is palpable even if it's not tactile. In that same way, a horse feels what is inside of every person they encounter even if the person doesn't touch them. I had a young Thoroughbred filly years ago who was very sensitive, and I remember one time I had a new farrier come to my farm to trim my horses' feet. This filly was in her stall and the farrier walked into her stall to put the halter on her and she threw herself against the stall wall and began to tremble with total fear in her eye. It turned out this farrier was a very rough, *show 'em who's boss* kind of guy, and this filly felt that in full force before he ever laid a hand on her. She knew exactly what was in his heart and she reacted to it. Interestingly enough I didn't recognize that about him until she showed me. I took him at his word (he claimed to be quiet and gentle with young horses) and I failed to *feel* who he really was—but it was very obvious to her.

It's important to be aware of the feel you present to a horse all the time, because the feel you present will dictate the response/s you receive. Not all horses need the same feel from a person, which is why it's important to be able to read a horse accurately. One horse will need to feel the human is confident and in charge; another horse will need to feel the human is non-threatening; another horse will need to feel the human is willing to cooperate; while another will need to feel the human presents clear directions and parameters, etc. Each horse has a different *feel need*, but all horses will react to us according to the feel they receive from us. The horse will be aware of the feel behind every aid we give. They can feel the anger or frustration in a rein aid just as clearly as they can feel the love and encouragement that comes from the human heart through the hand to the rein. They can feel whether our aids are punitive, or encouraging. They can feel whether we want the best for them, or whether we merely want to dominate them. They can feel what's inside of us better than we can sometimes, and this can lead to our frustration. I think sometimes we don't realize the feel we present to a horse, so we become angry or frustrated when he responds in a way we do not desire. This relates back to the conflict that can exist between our intellect and our emotions. If we intellectually want a horse to do something, but we are emotionally afraid, we will send a conflicted feeling to the horse. Then he has to decide which feel to respond to, and since we are conflicted there's a good chance he won't please us no matter what he does.

Other people are emotionally distraught within themselves and they use animals as an outlet to vent their own inner anger, frustration, or hurt. Many people believe animals are here on Earth to serve our needs, but that doesn't mean they are here to be the unwilling recipients of our own inner turmoil. We shouldn't be dealing with animals if we have severe unresolved emotional issues. Or at the very least, we shouldn't blame the animal for responding honestly to our inner failing.

- **Drive/Draw**

A good example of the importance of intent lies in the concepts of drive vs. draw, which are two different dynamics. The drive dynamic involves moving or sending a horse out of a space, and the draw dynamic involves asking him to come into a space. They are both valuable tools and at their core they address two different qualities we want to instill in a horse—i.e. respect and trust. A horse who respects us will move away from us (out of our space), and a horse who trusts us will move toward us (into our space). It's important that there be a fluid balance between the two. A horse lacking in trust will be too quick to get out of our way, and his fear level will be too high. A horse lacking respect will walk all over us and invade our space uninvited. We want to balance trust with respect and vice versa, and we can use drive and draw to help achieve that. But the point is that drive and draw require two different underlying intentions. On the one hand, we encourage or motivate a horse to leave a space (drive), and on the other we invite him to enter a space (draw). Our body language will vary depending on which intention we hold.

As an example, I have long heard that when lunging a horse we must not let our position get ahead of the horse's shoulder because it will block his forward movement. However, I frequently get out ahead of a horse when lunging, but I do it with a draw (vs. a drive) intent. I think of the lunge line like the string on a toy train and I apply a pressure which is essentially a forward pulling pressure. My intent is to invite the horse to come forward into the pressure which will cause him to align his body like the cars of the toy train will line up once the train is being pulled forward from the string. It's a very effective tactic (and works extremely well for alignment issues), but it requires a different intent and hence a different body language than when I stay behind the horse's shoulder and drive him forward.

- **The Bear**

Many years ago I saw a man do a demonstration in which he carved a bear out of a tree stump with a chainsaw. He was very skillful and everyone watching was impressed. Then someone asked him how he did it. His answer was *"Well...I take a stump of wood and my chainsaw, and I cut away everything that ISN'T a bear."* At the time I thought to myself *"Well, aren't you clever! Now we all know how to carve a bear out of a tree stump!"* (NOT) But his words stuck with me, and the more I thought about them the more I realized that even though his words gave us no idea as to the actual skills or techniques required to use a chainsaw on a block of wood, they did refer to his underlying intent. And as far as intent is concerned, his words are valuable. What his words mean to me is that when he gets a block of wood, he devotes no attention, no focus, and no energy to the part of the wood that is not a bear. Instead, all of his attention, all of his focus, and all of his energy is only on finding and releasing the bear within the stump of wood. He literally lets everything that isn't a bear fall to the ground as so much sawdust.

So how does that relate to training horses? It means that when we're working with a horse, we need to keep our sights on what we want—the bear—and not on what we don't want—what isn't a bear. If a horse is anxious and jigging instead of calmly walking as we ride him back to the barn from a trail ride, the jigging is not the bear. The bear—the thing we need to focus our attention and energy on—is gaining a calm, flat-footed walk. But many riders will get caught up trying to prevent the horse from jigging; they get caught up in what isn't a bear. They need to ignore the jigging, let the jigging *fall away* like all the pieces of wood that aren't a bear, and keep their sights, feel and focus (underlying intention) on creating a relaxed walk.

Whatever we focus our attention and our energies on in life will magnify, so if we focus our attention and energies on all those things we do not want we will actually expand their existence in our reality. There are times in life when we find things we weren't actively looking for, and many times those findings are valuable, but we usually discover those cherished surprise windfalls when our minds are open. If our minds are closed and our focus is on all that isn't a bear, that's all we'll ever find or experience in life. If we open our minds and put our focus on the things we want in life and from our horses, then we dramatically increase our chances of finding and/or achieving them.

If someone has a preconceived notion that their horse is a defiant jerk, they will be looking for all the ways their horse is a defiant jerk, and their horse will show them all the ways he can be. That person will create a horse who is a defiant jerk. But if someone else works with that same horse and holds the image of a calm, receptive, compliant animal in mind, they will dramatically increase their chances of the horse becoming calm, receptive and compliant.

Another way to imagine this is to think of it as *holding the vision between reality and possibility.* The reality is the uncut stump of wood, and the possibility is the finished statue of the bear, and within that context the woodcutter constantly holds the vision of the bear throughout the process of cutting the stump of wood. With horses, let's say the reality is that the horse is tense, anxious, and easily frustrated, and the possibility is that he becomes calm, relaxed, and patient. What we need to do in our dealings with him is hold the vision of the horse we want him to be even when he isn't—especially when he isn't. As soon as we lose our vision, we get caught up in the reality and the reality is not what we want—what we want is the possibility of what could be, so we want to hold the vision of the possibility as we deal with the reality.

These are different ways of thinking of one's underlying intentions and expectations, but be aware that gaining control and clarity of our underlying intentions and expectations, and making sure they take into account the well-being of the horse and his nature will have a huge positive impact on our dealings with our horses. We are the one carving the bear out of the stump of wood that is our horse, and like the woodcutter, it is in our own best interest to put our focus and energy on carving something we actually want.

· The Pendulum Swing

When changing behavior patterns, there occurs what I think of as a *pendulum swing*. If you visualize a pendulum at rest, it will be at center. Then if you take it to one side and let it go it will swing past center as it swings to the other side. The distance the pendulum swings on either side of center will be close to equal—it will swing to the right almost as far past center as it started out on the left. Eventually the swing range will dwindle down and it will go less and less far past center until it comes to rest at center. Behavioral changes can display a similar pendulum swing. For example, if a horse has been internalizing fear, frustration, and/or resentment because he's afraid to exhibit his emotional turmoil and then he is suddenly allowed to express his emotions, he may display those pent up emotions to the extreme. While he is internalizing his emotional turmoil, his behavior seems quiet and calm, though he is only quiet on the outside—he is actually distraught on the inside. But when he is allowed to exhibit his emotions, his behavior can change from seemingly quiet to troubled and turbulent, so he swings to the opposite side of center in his behavior. The extent to which his behavior becomes exaggerated will be almost a mirror image of the extent of the emotional turmoil he was previously holding inside or internalizing.

It's easy think when we begin the process of freeing the horse of emotional turmoil that he will go from troubled to tranquil and that will be the end of it, but his behavior will likely display a pendulum swing past center to the other side. In that sense, his emotional turmoil is the same, but his behavior may get worse before it gets better. It's also not uncommon to see a noticeable initial improvement, but then encounter a backslide as the work continues. I have on many occasions made big improvements with horses in just one session, but it's carrying those improvements over into his daily routine that takes time and patience, and backsliding can occur during that process, though if you look at the training overall you should see progress.

*Training is not something that occurs once and for all.
It occurs in a million little different ways in
a million little different interactions over a period of time.*

    Unfortunately some owners will see the big improvements that can be achieved initially and they'll think the horse is *fixed*. Then they become frustrated with the horse or upset with themselves when those improvements don't continue as readily as they did initially. We must remember it is a process, and the improvement can occur in a *two steps forward, one step back* type progression, but overall we should see a positive progression.

    I bought a horse a number of years ago who was a good example of the pendulum swing. His seller's situation was a weird one, to say the least, but suffice it to say when I went to look at him he had been confined to a stall for four months with no turnout or riding. I wanted to let him get any kinks out before riding him, and I also wanted to watch him move freely, so I turned him loose in their outdoor arena. At the time I was surprised at how quiet he was. He didn't run or buck as I had expected, but rather calmly walked around sniffing the ground. He was completely unruffled about being outside the confinement of his stall. I figured if he was that quiet after four months of stall confinement, he must be truly placid, but I grossly misjudged his actions.

    I brought him home to my farm where he had access to all day pasture turnout with other horses, and I started riding him, and slowly his true personality began to emerge. What I had interpreted as being quiet was an erroneous diagnosis. I eventually realized he wasn't quiet at his other home, he was dull due to a complete lack of sensory stimulation for months on end. His initial behavior when turned out in their outdoor arena was similar to bringing a prisoner out of months of solitary confinement in a dark hole into the sunshine. He would need an adjustment period to return to normal, and the longer he was in solitary, the longer the adjustment time.

Over the course of several months on my farm this horse's attitude and behavior went through some real changes. The pendulum swing started off with him being so quiet he was almost disconnected to life, but then it swung so far to the other side that he became a frightened and yet overbearing bully. He fought with the other horses so much I had to separate him, and he was a nervous wreck under saddle. My ultimate goal was to get him *to center*, but I had to endure some wide swings of the pendulum before we got there. And during the process, the undesirable behaviors he exhibited were in direct proportion to all the emotions he had denied and internalized during his long stall confinement and mistreatment. Because the pendulum had been so far to one side of center for so long, it had to swing just as far to the other side before we could slowly work our way back to center. Most horses aren't as far off center as he was, fortunately, but when working through problems or issues with a horse there may be that pendulum swing from one side to the other before coming to center.

In summing up the importance of one's underlying intentions and expectations, I am reminded of a fable. I tried to find a source for it, but was unsuccessful. At any rate, here it is:

> *An Indian tribe had a herd of horses with many mares and a few stallions. One of the stallions was a beautiful animal, but very aggressive and none of the young braves could approach him. He would come running at them with teeth bared. The only member of the tribe who could catch and ride the stallion was the Old Chief. One day a Young Brave went to the Old Chief to find out his secret for getting the vicious stallion so tame. He asked the Old Chief how he was able to get the dangerous stallion to be so gentle. The Old Chief walked out of his tent and soon returned with a lock of hair tied with a leather thong. He handed*

it to the Young Brave and told him to hold it in his hand as he went out to capture the stallion and the stallion would be calm.

Early the next morning, before the other young braves were awake, he went to the herd holding his lock of hair and approached the stallion. The stallion acknowledged him, and he stopped. His heart was pounding as he feared the stallion could easily harm him as he'd never been so close to him before. But much to his surprise the stallion lowered his head and calmly walked up to him. He stroked the stallion's neck, then swung up onto his back and rode the stallion around. He was thrilled at how well the magic hair had worked. He did this every morning for a week, and the stallion was as docile as could be.

Then one morning as he was standing and waiting for the stallion to approach him a gust of wind blew the magic hair from his hand. In panic he began to retreat, and as he did the stallion began to charge. He ran to safety, but went directly to the tent of the Old Chief to get more magic hair. He told the chief how the hair had blown away and he needed more. The Old Chief said "Do you see that old blind mare over there? Go over and cut a lock of her tail hair". The Young Brave was furious and shouted at him "Do you mean the magic hair you gave me was from that old worthless mare?" The Old Chief looked at him and said "I never told you the hair was magic. The magic was in your belief".

Dominance & Submission

As humans with egos we are in love with the concept of superiority and/or dominance over others. It reinforces our sense of self in what we perceive to be an empowering manner. We like to be in control of everyone and everything, including our children, pets, and horses. The issue of dominance and its flip side, submission, is important in dealing with horses because they are large and pose a bigger potential threat than our small animals, but sometimes we address dominance over a horse in a counter-productive manner. We think of dominance in human terms, which are predatory in nature. In that sense, we think of dominance as our ability to restrain or control the flight of a horse, but horses view dominance the opposite of us. The dominant horse in a herd is the one who can move the other horse/s out of his space. Dominance to a horse has nothing to do with the ability to restrain another horse, rather it is about moving the feet of the other horse. If one horse pins his ears at another, and the second horse moves out of his way, the first horse is dominant and the second horse is submissive. Yet we tend to think we are dominant when we can control or prevent a horse's flight instinct, and the horse is submissive when he stops trying to flee. What we perceive as our dominance and the horse's submission is actually the prey giving up in the clutches of the predator to the horse's way of thinking.

To avoid the predator/prey conflict, the way we obtain authority and establish our dominance in our interactions with horses is worth thoughtful consideration. Horses can be very rough with one another if need be. We've all seen a horse turn around and kick another horse with both hind feet to make him move, but that doesn't mean we should use similar tactics. I differentiate between *command* and *demand*. The difference may be one of semantics, but I believe the feeling behind the difference is important. *Command*, to me, means

I fully expect something, though it's not an absolute in the moment. It's the sense that I know ultimately I will prevail, but it may or may not occur this moment, or even today. I think of command as coming from my own inner conviction—such as I command a horse's respect. *Demand* means insistence by any means, and it means NOW. I like the saying *speak softly but carry a big stick*.[3] The big stick is one's underlying intentions and expectations, which need to be rock solid, then we can use smaller, quieter physical actions in our interaction. In that sense, I think of command as coming from the *inside*, and demand referring to bigger physical actions which come from the *outside*. We are less likely to trigger resistance or opposition in our horses if we command vs. demand.

Horses are designed to live in a hierarchical society and submission is a necessary ingredient. The question is in how it is obtained. Submission is an internal state of being. A horse is submissive to a human because he *thinks* he is. Does he think that because his dominant behaviors are punished? or because he has been brought to that state of being through a more subtle approach? For example, dominance to a horse is about who moves whose feet, and you can move a horse's feet in a very subtle manner and still get the point across. I see owners grooming their horses, and the horse swings his rear end around and the owner moves out of the way, or the horse swings his head around and the human ducks. They do little things like that 15 times before they get to the mounting block and then wonder why their horse is not submissive when they ride him. The reason is because they showed him 15 times from the stall to the mounting block that he was dominant over them. Every time the horse moved into the human's space, and the human stepped away, the horse's dominance was reinforced.

If a horse invades our space all that is needed is to re-position his feet—i.e. back him up, or move him over—but a more aggressive handler might take that horse and slap his chest back and forth with the lead rope as he backs him down the aisle way 50 feet. He demands respect and that horse will then follow him in a very subdued manner, and will do his best to stay out of his way in the future. That method can *work* on the level of behavior, but it doesn't create behavior/s that arises from a calm, willing inner composure and it doesn't always carry over to a more passive human. I see many horses who have learned to *stay under the radar* with an aggressive trainer, but once they realize that not all humans are equal, a few of them will actually impose their internal frustration and/or resentment on the humans they perceive to be weaker—often the owners. Many of those owners then think the trainer needs to beat up their horse even more, but what I see is that the trainer's aggressive approach is causing the problems to begin with. The horses are afraid of the trainer, but they swallow their fear, and then unleash their frustration on their more passive owners.

Through constant awareness we can often preempt unwanted behaviors or immediately make small corrections, but many owners don't want to have to think about what they do, much less take responsibility for it. The thing is you don't create submission once and for all. You create it in a million little different ways throughout a horse's lifetime. When you first open his stall door, does he turn his tail to you? or turn to face you? If he turns his tail, I don't walk into the stall, rather I flick the end of the lead rope at his rump until he turns to face me. Then I stand there and wait for him to approach. If he's hesitant to approach (lacking trust) I'll back up. As I lead him out to the cross ties I am aware of every step he takes. If even one step is too close to me I will make him conscious of it by stopping and moving him over. Initially I will spend as much time as necessary tacking up an ill-mannered horse because I will constantly show him that he needs to be aware of me and to adjust his feet to where I am, not the other way around. So respect and submission are instilled literally one step, or one tiny move, at a time.

Dominance and submission are a way of life—not an absolute, and not something that is determined once and for all. If we will systematically teach the behaviors of submission then the inner state of submission soon follows. But if the behaviors of submission are taught too harshly, or the lack of submission punished, then the inner state of being will not be one of calm composure. So the key very much lies in how it is done.

Back in the 1980's I used to buy and sell Thoroughbreds off the racetrack. I bought an older gelding (7 or 8 years old) who had been used as a pony horse. He would take 10 to 12 colts out on the track everyday to gallop, and he had marks on the right side of his neck and chest where the colts would bite him. I suspect the gelding thought the colts were ill-mannered and impudent, but I also suspect his rider would not allow him to retaliate, so he learned to swallow his frustration. I bought him and wanted to let him go to pasture every day with my other geldings, but he was so aggressive I was afraid to leave him unsupervised. I continued to ride him, and his training improved, but I finally realized that although he was not aggressive with me I needed to somehow address his dominance with the other horses. Time in a herd will often sort out these issues, but it didn't with him.

So I started doing some dominance/submission related ground work with him asking him to move his feet, mainly sideways and backwards as he was already very forward thinking. I made a point to always ask politely and softly, and he would do it, but not *happily*. And every time I turned him out after our sessions he would gallop away from me and aggressively go after one of the other horses with ears pinned and teeth bared. His aggression seemed to be worse when I was doing those sessions even though I was careful not to fight with him in any way, and I was consciously trying to assert my dominance politely. I was being as even-keeled and quiet as I could be. Then one day he had a relapse, for whatever reason, and he wouldn't move over—it was like his feet had grown roots. I stood there and asked again with the lightest touch on his shoulder, but he remained stuck. So then I told him, in actual words, *"You can stand here as long as you like, but we aren't leaving until you move over. If you want to stay here until next Tuesday, that's fine with me. I can be just as stubborn as you"*. And we both just stood there staring at each other. After a few moments he dropped his head, let out a big sigh, and began to lick and chew. At the time I wasn't sure what to make of that, but he seemed to be more compliant. (He was also the horse who taught me the power of releasing tension/anxiety). After he did that, he moved over readily and I led him to the pasture to turn him out. This time when I removed his halter he quietly stood beside me instead of galloping off. I stroked his neck for a minute and then I turned around and walked away from him. When he went out to the herd he didn't run, but walked calmly, and for the first time he didn't go after another horse aggressively. That day was a turning point for him (and for me). I owned him another 2 years waiting for the right person to buy him, and although he was always the dominant horse in the herd, he changed in that one day from being aggressively dominant to being a benevolent dictator, if you will. It was as if he had internalized the example I was trying to set of being politely dominant.

Since then I have used that as a gauge of my success—i.e. I watch how a horse leaves me and returns to the herd as an indication of whether I have truly *gotten to the bottom of him* or not. Often when I start dominance/submission work, even though it is quiet and non-confrontational, the horses will do one of two things: 1) gallop away from me and immediately look for another horse to bully, or 2) gallop off as they whinny looking for the security of the herd situation. But after a few sessions they begin to change—they calmly walk away and there is no retaliation against their herd members, or there is not the frantic need for reassurance. I have noticed the work can quiet the actions of an aggressive horse, but it can also increase the confidence of a timid horse. So just because horses do things naturally doesn't mean they can't change with our handling. I have seen many horses make big changes in their interactions with other horses as a result of their training sessions. It has become a gauge to me as to how I'm doing. Dominance and submission are an integral part of a horse's life, but that doesn't mean we can't change how they naturally deal with those issues. I know my training is on the right track when my horses are calm, quiet and polite with each other the 23 hours a day they aren't working with me.

The Flip Side of the Coin

In many instances with horses, and other situations in life, I've found my answers or solutions by flipping the coin over and looking at it from the other side. One example of what I think of as the flip side of the coin involves the issue of human health care. Conventional medicine approaches health care from the standpoint of either preventing and/or treating illness or injury, while alternative medicine approaches the issue from the standpoint of promoting wellness. Both are ultimately concerned with one's health and well-being, yet they are very different approaches. They are flip sides of the same coin, with one approach being proactive while the other approach is often reactive. Theoretically, if one did a good enough job of promoting his own wellness (a proactive approach), then he would not need the services of a doctor to treat his ills (a reactive approach). Notice I said theoretically. I'm certainly not saying anything against modern medicine, but if everyone took a judicious approach to promoting their own wellness there would be less illness to treat. At any rate, the same type of thinking applies to horse training as well. We are either proactive in our training or reactive.

There are many things we teach horses that we can approach from either a standpoint of causing him to *get away* from one thing or we can teach him to *go to* something else. *Going to* vs. *getting away from* are flip sides of the same coin, yet which one we put our focus on will have a dramatic influence on the outcome. When a horse is motivated to get away from one thing, there isn't anything specific he's going to, rather his only aim is to get away from whatever it is that is troubling, or frightening to him. Showing him how to *go to* something is much more specific and contains a clearer objective for him to understand.

For example, a bit can be used either as a means of control or a means of communication, and those two things are not necessarily compatible. Control can be gained through pain. The horse who is afraid to touch the bit because of the pain inflicted by it will hold his mouth back off the bit. That horse might feel soft to the rider's hands, but he's only soft because he's trying to avoid the pain of the bit. On the other hand, the rider who uses the bit as a means of communication will offer the bit to the horse in a way that encourages him to understand the rider's request. That rider will use the bit to show the horse how to *go to* whatever his desire is. As a means of communication the bit will not be an absolute means of control, but will rather exert an influence on the horse based on the degree of communication that is built around it—i.e. the greater the communication, the greater the influence, and in that sense, the greater the control.

The difference can also be described as one of training by design vs. training by default. If we train by design, we have a very clear idea of our objective, and our actions are designed to show the horse what that objective is and how to achieve it. Yet some riders think training is about simply telling the horse *"No, that's wrong"* every time he does something wrong. So if he does 50 things wrong, they tell him *"No, that's wrong"* 50 times, but he still doesn't know what is right! He may accidentally stumble on the right response, and then his rider will quit nagging or punishing him, and in that manner he can learn how to escape the criticism, but he's still not actively seeking the right response in the positive sense. It's more that he's escaping the criticism by offering the behavior that causes it to cease—so even though his response is correct, he's *escaping to correctness*, and his reaction (even though it's the right one) is offered by default rather than by design. If he is made to understand the right response, and he's encouraged to exhibit it, and he's rewarded when he does, then his training is by design and he is given something clear and concrete to go to. Good training is more about *direction* than it is about *correction*, and yet the opposite is too often seen.

As another example, say a horse is anxious and always goes too fast—even when he's walking, he walks too fast. Note there is a difference between a free swinging, ground-covering walk born of relaxation and a quick, hurried walk born of anxiety. I am referring to the latter. In that context, we can look at this and approach it from two different viewpoints:

1) We can tell the horse *no* every time he speeds up. We might say that to him by holding onto the reins tighter, or even jerking the bit in his mouth—but our focus is on telling him *"NO—don't go fast."*—or,

2) We can put our focus on encouraging him to go slow.

It might seem this is six of one, half a dozen of the other, but the difference between having our focus on not having him go fast vs. encouraging him to go slow is important. If we simply don't want him to go fast, first of all, that isn't really giving him an alternative. Saying to him *"No, don't go fast"* doesn't give him a clear idea of what we do want and expect from him. It might seem obvious to the person, but it is not to the horse. When all we say is *"Don't go fast"*, then if he does go slow, he has done so by accident. He has managed to figure out on his own that he can escape criticism or punishment if he slows down. He may not be emotionally okay with going slow, but he's found that slowness is a place he can *escape to*. So even if he does go slow, he's doing so because he's getting away from the criticism or punishment when he goes fast.

But if we say to him *"Go slow"*, then our intent will be to encourage him to slow down, and that intent will come through our body language and our feel sense. Our actions will be the ones that will encourage slowness through a presented feeling of inner quiet and calm, and in that sense we will be training him by design. We will be showing him exactly what it is we do want from him, and we will be feeling within ourselves what it is we want to feel from him. Chances are the reason he is too fast to begin with is because he's feeling anxious or nervous or fearful, and his means of dealing with fear or anxiety is to get away from it. If his rider only addresses his actions by trying to prevent him from going fast, or by punishing him for going fast, that won't change his inner state of being, and will actually enhance it.

It is also very common for a rider who opposes what the horse is doing to feel their own negative emotion within that opposition, such as frustration or anger. If the horse's inner state of being is calm and quiet, he won't try to get away from where he is and so he can easily slow down. A horse goes too fast because he wants to be someplace else, so he speeds up to get there. If he's content to be where he is, he will be content to go at whatever speed or pace suits his rider. So the rider needs to present the inner state of being he wants to elicit in the horse. The rider/handler needs to *feel* what he wants the horse to do, even when the horse isn't doing it—and especially when the horse isn't doing it.

Point of View

Imagine a circle of people standing around a dog who is sitting in the center of the circle. Since a circle is comprised of 360 degrees, let's say there are 360 people standing side by side on this circle. Then visualize the circle like the face of a clock, with the dog facing 12:00. Each and every person will have a different point of view of the dog, and the point of view of the person standing at 12:00 will be diametrically opposed to the point of view of the person standing at 6:00. If you were to ask the person standing at 12:00 to describe what he sees, he will describe a face with eyes, ears, nose and mouth, a chest, part of a belly, and two front feet. But the person standing at 6:00 will describe the back of two ears, the back of a head, the back of the dog, a tail, and the seated haunches. They might both even see different colors depending on the coloring of the dog. The people standing at 3:00 and 9:00 will describe a similar animal as they are both viewing the dog from the side. Their discrepancy, if any, would likely only be color if the dog was irregularly marked.

But the point is, is one of the people right in their description and the others wrong? And of course the answer is no. Each person sees what he sees depending on his particular perspective. However, say the person standing in front of the dog says to the person standing behind the dog *"You should see his face. It's so cute."* The only way the person standing behind the dog will be able to see his face is if he literally changes his point of view by walking around and looking at the dog from the front.

Sometimes people will literally change their point of view by physically moving so they see something from another angle, yet some of those same people might be very reluctant to figuratively change their point of view by *mentally seeing* something from another perspective. Those people get stuck in their perceptions and refuse to change them. If they think horses have small brains and are stupid, then they will *see* all horses as being stupid. They will also expect horses to act in ways they consider to be stupid, and they will gear all their interactions with horses to suit and support the horse's supposed stupidity. So to them the horse is a stupid animal, and that perception will surely be validated because they will be looking for nothing other than stupidity in horses.

But if they were to merely change their perspective and perceive horses as thinking, feeling, sensitive animals capable of rational thought and even individual opinions, their interactions with horses will be dramatically different. I saw a video series of interviews commentated by Bill Moyer called *The Power of the Myth* with Joseph Campbell, and in one of them Campbell was talking about Native Americans and their feelings toward buffalo. They revered the buffalo for contributing to their very survival, and to them the buffalo were highly valued. It was in reference to their perspective that Joseph Campbell said:

> *"The ego that sees a 'thou' is not the same ego that sees an 'it'. Your whole psychology changes when you address things as an 'it'."*

Thinking of another as *thou* carries with it respect and consideration for another living being. Thinking of another as *it* carries no such esteem or honor. Yet that simple change in perspective is capable of causing one to undergo a completely different experience in life. We all find what we seek in life, and yet we need to actively seek those things we want to find. If we believe in the dignity and glory of another we will surely have a different relationship with them than if we believe in their stupidity or lack of refinement, whether the other being is human or animal. Likewise, if we believe in the dignity and worthiness of all others, we will dramatically change our entire life experience. Isn't it sad that the only thing standing between a life of grandeur and a life of narrow-minded limitations is one's point of view? It's all a matter of perspective.

Punishment vs. Reward

Our underlying intentions and expectations set the stage for what it is we want to achieve in our horse training, and their value is immeasurable to our success or failure, but once we have a clear grasp of our intentions and expectations, we still need to utilize working tools to achieve them. This process is called behavior modification and the tools fall into one of two general categories:
1) Desired behaviors are reinforced and/or rewarded, and
2) Undesired behaviors are discouraged and/or punished.
Simply stated, the behaviors we want are encouraged, and the behaviors we don't want are discouraged. With that in mind, these two categories were further broken down by B. F. Skinner in his studies on operant conditioning. To encourage the behaviors we want, we can use:
  a. Positive Reinforcement, or
  b. Negative Reinforcement

And to discourage the behaviors we don't want, we can use:
  c. Positive Punishment, or
  d. Negative Punishment

In regard to behavior modification, the words *positive* and *negative* refer to something either being added (positive) to the equation, or something taken away (negative). They do not mean positive and negative in the sense of good or bad. Many people think negative reinforcement means punishment because of the word negative, but that is a misperception. For example, say my horse is walking along and I want him to trot. I squeeze my calves against his sides until he trots, and as soon as he does, I quit squeezing. That's a common example of negative reinforcement—i.e. I present an aid (the squeezing of my legs), and I take it away (the negative part) as soon as the desired behavior is exhibited. In that sense I reinforce the behavior I am seeking by showing the horse that if he trots when I squeeze my legs I will quit squeezing. Since he would like for me to quit squeezing my legs, he learns to go faster when I do. Then as soon as he trots, I can tell him *"Good boy"*, and stroke his neck. That is positive reinforcement—i.e. I add something (the verbal and physical praise) once the behavior has been exhibited to further reinforce it. So both negative and positive reinforcement are concerned with encouraging and/or rewarding those behaviors we want.

Negative reinforcement is an integral part of horse training. It can always be followed with positive reinforcement, but negative reinforcement is utilized any time we give the horse an aid or cue and we quit cuing as soon as he does what we want. Negative reinforcement creates a release for the horse when he does what we want, and if we use it properly we encourage the horse to *seek the release*. In that sense, it is not the cue, per se, that teaches the horse what we want, rather it is the release of the cue. We could, if so inclined, flick a horse's left ear to mean we want a right lead canter. If we quick flicking when he picks up a right lead canter he will eventually learn what the cue means, even though the cue itself has no inherent meaning to him. He learns what the cue means from the release of it. Bear in mind there is a distinct, albeit subtle, difference between a horse seeking a release and one simply avoiding pressure. Seeking a release ties in with *going to* something, while avoiding pressure is simply *getting away from* it.

A horse seeks a release in the good sense because he has become an interactive partner in his own training, and he has learned there is a right answer to every question posed by the human. He has learned he will find the release once he finds the right answer. A key component in this process is that he will be much more inclined to actively seek a release if he is not punished for the wrong answer/s in the process of finding the right one! That is an important concept to be aware of. He can quickly stop trying to find any answer if his wrong answers are punished.

When people punish the wrong answer they think they are punishing the behavior, but to the horse it is his try—his attempt—that is being punished. If his try is punished enough, he'll quit trying.

Avoiding pressure, on the other hand, is not interactive, rather it is a horse's way of disconnecting from the training process. For example, if a horse feels pain from the bit in his mouth, he will learn to quickly avoid the pain by tucking his head down and inward, but that horse is not actively seeking the meaning of the pressure of the bit, he is merely avoiding the pain caused by it. That horse never truly leaves his *primitive brain* [4] because he is always on the defensive. The aids used can be lighter with the horse who actively seeks a release, because he is an interactive, thinking partner. If he is only avoiding pressure, the pressure can too often become actual pain in order to cause the horse to avoid it. At that point the pressure has lost any meaning. So negative reinforcement encourages the behaviors we desire, and positive reinforcement rewards those behaviors when the horse exhibits them, but the important thing to note is they both address those behaviors we want. If used with care, they cause the horse to become involved in his own training and they instill in him a desire to find the right answer and/or to seek the release.

The other category consists of positive and negative punishment. Positive punishment is the kind seen most often. Again, the positive means something is added to discourage a behavior. For example, say a horse gets scared while being led and tries to take off (undesired behavior), so the handler jerks on a chain over his nose (i.e. he adds pain to the equation) to punish the horse for taking off; or a horse attempts to bite, so the handler hits him with a whip; or, a horse picks up the wrong canter lead so the rider pulls him back to a walk and spurs him into the canter again, etc. Those are all examples of positive punishment, but one thing to note is that positive punishment is always used *after* a behavior has been exhibited to discourage the horse from doing it again. In that sense, punishment is always reactive in nature, and always occurs after the fact. I've asked riders before why they punished their horse for something he did and they say *"Because I don't want him to think he can get away with doing that"*, and I say *"But he already did!"* What they hope will happen is the punishment will cause the horse to not do it again, but sometimes it causes the horse to become clever at avoiding punishment. And when it does *work* it will tend to shut down other behaviors as well—behaviors that are not objectionable. I see many horses who *hide* in their work. Their contribution to the interaction becomes less and less forthcoming for fear of making a mistake. They perform like robots on automatic pilot, and while they are often seen as well-trained they are a sad sight to my eyes.

Having said all of that, there is one advantage to positive punishment, which is it is delivered quickly and often reactively by the rider, meaning it can be something to use in an emergency situation. I believe we should try to avoid using punishment in our everyday training, but in an emergency we need to do what we can do to be safe, and that might involve something perceived by the horse as punishing. Another more *acceptable* use of punishment is setting up a situation in which the horse associates his behavior with the punishment and does not view the human as the *punisher*. If we are continually perceived as the punisher*s* it can create fear or resentment in the horse, but we can bypass that perception if the horse associates only his behavior with the punishment. For example, say I'm leading a cheeky colt who wants to bite my arm. My elbow might accidentally (on purpose) jut out just as his mouth is coming in for a good nip, so the side of his muzzle bumps the bony point of my elbow. It will be uncomfortable for him, but I can act like I had nothing to do with it. I can even say *"Oh, I'm sorry. Did you hurt your mouth when you tried to bite me?"* But if I make it obvious that I am trying to punish the behavior—like if I waved my arm about trying to hit him for biting—he will very likely just get more clever at biting and quickly getting out of the way of my arm. So with prudence there can be occasions when we can set up a self-punishing situation to extinguish an unwanted behavior.

> *The worst part of positive punishment is the punitive feel that often accompanies it. We usually punish when we are angry or frustrated and we project an inner feeling of wanting to do harm to the horse so he won't do whatever* again.

If we use punishment as a training tool we need to think of it as a calm, rational, consistent consequence and not a reactive or defensive action intending to cause pain or harm. For example, if a horse is prone to taking off, the rider can calmly and consistently use one rein to bring him around to a very small circle, so the consequence of taking off is to take off onto a small circle which makes the taking off difficult. That calm, rational consequence is far preferable to jerking on the reins or inflicting pain for taking off.

Negative punishment isn't used as often, but it refers to something that is withheld or taken away in order to discourage a behavior. For example, if your horse kicks his stall at feeding time and you want to discourage that behavior you could withhold his food until he stops kicking. He learns that he won't get his food if he kicks (the food is taken away or withheld), so he stops the kicking (the undesired behavior). However, there can be a fine line between negative punishment and positive reinforcement. You could make the argument that you are using positive reinforcement in the above example because you will give him his food (adding a reward) when he's not kicking (the desired behavior).

At any rate, the most important aspect of the training tools—reinforcement and/or reward vs. discouragement and/or punishment—concerns our own focus. If our only training tool is punishment, then our focus will always be on those behaviors we do not want. Sort of like the old saying: *If all you have is a hammer, everything looks like a nail.* How can we use punishment as a training tool if we don't look for and find undesirable behaviors to punish? But if we flip the coin over and look at the other side we'll see that by using reward as our training tool, we will be actively looking for those behaviors we can reward. So which tool we use to train with, reward or punishment, will have a monumental impact on our entire interaction with our horses.

I remember a trail ride I took with a rider many years ago. I was riding a young mare and she was riding an older gelding. The day was idyllic—it was a crisp spring day following a nice rainfall the night before, so the grass was green, the sky was blue with a slight breeze in the air, and there was the smell and feeling of new life that early spring always harbors. I was losing myself in the feel of such a glorious day and at the same time I was aware of all that my young horse was experiencing for she had not been on a trail ride before. She was a little hesitant and curiously taking in all the sights and sounds, but overall she was very good. I took in all the ride had to offer in a similar fashion to the way she did—with an open awareness and feel of my surroundings. I frequently scratched her on the withers as if to say "*good girl*", and I believe we both enjoyed the ride.

My friend, however, had a very different experience. For one thing, her mind was not on the ride or the scenery at all. She was having trouble at home and her personal troubles were all she could think about. We rode about an hour and during that time her gelding looked at something three different times. I can't even say he spooked because his reaction was no more than a hiccup, but several times she felt him hesitate for a second before he proceeded. Each time he did that she became upset and asked me what he was looking at. At one point she chided him for it. When we finished the ride she made the comment that her horse had been spooky the whole time. From my point of view her horse had hesitated a second or two at three different times out of an hour ride, so no more than six seconds total. He was perfectly fine the other 59 minutes and 54 seconds. Yet the only time she paid any attention to him was when he hesitated, so her only awareness of him was those six seconds. She never once commended him for all he had done that was good. Her mind and focus was never on her horse, so the only time he gained her attention was when he did something she considered *bad*. This type of situation is extremely common in horse training (as well as life in general). Allowing unwanted behaviors or situations to capture our attention is easy because we can let our minds wander until the unwanted situation brings us back to awareness of the horse. Being aware of and rewarding good behaviors, however, requires us to constantly be mentally connected to the interaction. In order to acknowledge all the times when a horse does something good we must truly be *in the moment*. And many times what is *good* is simply the absence of what is *bad*. It is very easy to take the good behaviors of horses for granted. If a horse is calmly walking down the trail that is a good thing, and yet it is also rather mundane and easy to take for granted. It hardly seems worth acknowledging or rewarding, and yet we need to look for all those ways in which our horses get along with us, regardless of how unexceptional they may seem. A little appreciation and acknowledgement for seemingly insignificant things can go a long way toward creating a willing and reliable partner in our horse.

The best way for us to focus on what we want is to use encouragement and reward as our training tools, because then we will be actively looking for those behaviors we desire. Using punishment as a training tool causes us to focus on everything we don't want, or it allows us to ignore what is happening until the horse does something bad to snap us back to awareness. Using encouragement and reward to train is *training by design*. Using prevention or punishment is *training by default* because the horse only learns how to avoid punishment, and he does that by eventually figuring out how to escape it. If he escapes to the right answer, he learns how to *escape to correctness*, but it's still escape; it's still a desire to not *be with* the human in the moment.

If we train our horses using encouragement and reward, then we will need in our mind a clear understanding of what it is we want him to do. That is step one. Often times riders use punishment as their training tool because they don't really have a clear idea within themselves of what they are trying to achieve; they only know what they don't want. They know they want the horse to do *something*, but they're not exactly sure what, so they punish everything that isn't what they think they want. I guess the hope is the horse will eventually figure it out, but since we are supposed to be the more intelligent species it seems logical that we ought to have it figured out before we attempt to teach it to the horse. But if we are not exactly sure what it is we're trying to achieve, it's all the more important we don't use positive punishment in the process! We need to try to at least keep our focus on what it is we think we want, and then analyze the horse's responses in terms of how they fit our perceived model or vision.

Using reinforcement as a training tool doesn't mean we never increase the physical or mental pressure we put on a horse. Negative reinforcement relies on our ability to somehow cause the behavior to happen so we can then reward it through release and/or praise. And sometimes we need to strongly motivate a horse to do whatever it is we want him to do in order to reward him. To the untrained eye there can be a blurry line between motivation and punishment, and sometimes the only difference is one's underlying intention/s. For example, consider the following two scenarios:

1. A handler is leading a horse and the horse barges ahead of him so he jerks down on the halter three times.
2. A handler is leading a horse and the horse barges ahead of him so he jerks down on the halter three times.

You might think I mistyped the above, but I did not. There can be two scenarios that look just the same on the surface, but are in fact quite different in intent. In situation #1, the handler used the jerks on the halter to punish the horse. The horse barged past him which angered him, so he began to jerk on the halter. His first jerk caused the horse's head to fly upward as he continued to barge forward. His second jerk caused the horse to stop. His third jerk caused the horse to begin to back up quickly in fear. His idea was to punish the horse's barging so he wouldn't do it again. He then continued to lead the horse forward while looking for any sign the horse might want to barge ahead so he could be quicker to punish him for it.

Handler #2, however, had a different motive in mind. His goal was not to punish the barging but to motivate the horse to go slow. So when the horse barged ahead, he jerked down once on the halter and the horse's head flew upward as he continued to barge. His second jerk caused the horse to slow down—which was the beginning of the behavior he wanted. His third jerk was not as firm as the first two yet caused the horse to stop, which he praised as he released all pressure on the horse and allowed him to stand still for a moment. He then continued to lead the horse forward while fully intending and expecting him to walk calmly by his side.

The thing to note is handler #1 continued to jerk on the halter after the horse had already stopped and even begun to back up, so from the horse's point of view he was being punished for stopping and backing up. The handler thought he was punishing him for his initial barging ahead, but his punitive approach caused him to continue to apply the punishment even after the horse had begun to comply with the request. I've seen many cases where punishment is continued even after the horse has quit the offensive behavior and is doing the right thing. If Handler #2 had been leading horse #1 he would have quit jerking on the halter after the second time, because that was when the horse quit barging. That was the time to praise the correct response, but the nature of punishment often entails additional usage. It causes us to approach things with a punitive edge or feel to our actions and we want to make sure the horse *never does that again*. In trying to make that point loud and clear it's common to overdo punishment.

At any rate, you can see that two seemingly similar situations are really very different. The difference is one of intent and timing on the part of the handler. The handler who is using punishment as his training tool is not as concerned with the behavior he wants as he is with punishing the behavior he doesn't want. For that reason, he's likely to continue to punish even after the horse is exhibiting the behavior he does want, and at that point, the horse is being punished for doing what the handler would want (if the handler actually thought about what he wanted and not gotten lost in what he didn't want).

Punishment always occurs after the fact, so the timing of punishment is not aimed at making it clear to the horse what IS desired. In addition, using punishment gives the human's actions a punitive feel, and many horses will come to resent or resist that feel. Often times the horse will resist the person strictly based on that punitive feel and the resistance can have nothing to do with what the person thinks he is doing. Rather the horse senses the punitive aspect of the human's demeanor and his defenses swell up. This interaction can become a vicious cycle between human and horse, because it causes the horse to become defensive, and often it is the behaviors that arise from defensiveness that the human feels the need to punish.

The second handler used the downward jerk on the lead line to motivate the horse to do what he wanted—i.e. stay by his side. Since his intent was different, his timing was too. He quit jerking the instant the horse began to slow and he then he focused on causing the horse to stop so he was beside him again and not out in front of him. The intent and timing of his actions were focused on what he wanted and on showing the horse what that was. His feel was one of encouragement, so the horse got a whole different feel sense from him than from the punitive handler even though he applied pressure in the process.

There are other ways of dealing with a horse who barges ahead of you when you lead him than the above example, but the example was aimed at showing how seemingly similar actions can come from very different underlying intentions.

- For the horse that barges ahead, you can teach him to back up from a light feel on the lead line from a halt. You can also practice walking forward 3 steps, backward 1-3 steps, forward 3 steps, backward 1-3 steps, etc., until he gets to where he begins to prepare himself to back up AS you walk him forward. If he's preparing to back up when going forward, he won't be barging forward, rather he'll be balanced over all 4 feet waiting for the signal to back up. Then you can increase the number of forward steps before asking for the back up.
- Another option would be to walk him along an arena wall and if he barges forward, turn him in front of you so he goes three-quarters of a circle around you and into the wall so you let the wall stop him. Praise him when he stops (even though he had no choice because he ran into the wall), then continue. Every time he barges forward, turn him so he goes into the wall. Pretty soon he'll catch on.
- Or you can carry a whip in your outside hand and as you lead him you can wave the whip up and down in front of

his face if he gets too fast. You can tie a small flag onto the end of the whip to make it more compelling.

- You can also turn around and quickly walk the other way as soon as he gets too quick.

But the point is all of these options are designed to show the horse that you want him to stay by your side, and not simply to punish him for barging ahead. They are designed to change his behavior, not merely punish it.

First Impulse

In our training, the first thing we need to focus on is the horse's *first impulse*. That is his very first reaction to what we do, and when I say very first, I mean the reaction that occurs in the first instant following a request. For example, say you're trying to teach your young horse to lead so you apply a light pressure to his halter and he raises his head, pulls back and begins to step back away from you. His first impulse is to tighten his back and under neck muscles which allow him to raise his head and the subsequent actions are the pulling back and stepping back, yet it is the first impulse we need to change. Many times, people will go to battle with a horse over all the things he does after his first impulse, but if we can change his first impulse, we are well on our way to changing the entire interaction.

With the young horse, we could start by teaching him to release his back and under neck muscles by dropping his head and neck down. This can be done before actual leading—sort of a precursor to leading. Once he learns that response we can pair it with a light pressure to the halter, so when we ask him to step forward his first response will be to relax his back and neck. Then we can ask for a step forward with a relaxed neck, and reward any compliance. Or another approach would be to simply maintain the same light but consistent pressure on the halter and go along with him as he raises his head and backs up. He won't back up forever, and when he realizes that 1) pulling back isn't making the pressure go away, and 2) we aren't threatening to him, he will begin to look for another option. At that point, he might lower his head of his own accord. When he does that, it should ease the pressure on his halter which is a reward in itself (negative reinforcement), and then we can couple that with verbal or physical praise (positive reinforcement).

We want to be able to apply a light pressure to the halter and have the horse move into it so it goes away and he finds a release. If we remain calm and in our thinking brain we can get through to him just what it is we want him to do, which is yield forward or downward to pressure on his halter as his first impulse. Once we change his first impulse, then teaching him to lead will be easier. What happens more commonly is the first impulse slips by unnoticed, and we end up in a fight with him over his subsequent reactions (raising his head and/or pulling or stepping back). Then it can turn into a situation where he becomes defensive over our strong-arm techniques and the initial issue, which is yielding forward into a release, gets lost in the battle. Anytime we ask anything of a horse, we need to pay close attention to his first impulse. If his first impulse is compliance, we have a springboard from which to carry that onward. But if his first impulse is non-compliance, then we need to stay right at that point and try to change that first impulse instead of going to battle over what will follow. Finding the first impulse is really only a matter of being more acutely aware of the horse's reaction/s, and identifying what he does AS he begins to do it. Most negative first impulses begin as an instinctive and/or defensive reaction. Once we become aware we can begin to identify his reaction/s while they are still in this stage, and through guidance we can show him how to change the resulting action through a sequence in which he stays connected to the interaction and thinks his way through it.

I remember a horse I got in for training a number of years ago, and his problem is a good example of recognizing the first impulse. He was sent to me as being dull, lazy, and unresponsive to the leg aids in addition to which he had begun to rear when asked to go forward. So the first time I got on him, I paid very close attention to his first impulse to everything I asked of him. When I focused my attention on his very first impulse, I realized that when he felt even the slightest hint of a leg aid, he pinned his ears and began to sull up. [5] I could feel that if I continued to apply more pressure that he would not go forward, and would likely rear. His reaction told me that he was not dull—quite the contrary! He was extremely sensitive. However, his reaction also told me he was exceedingly resentful of the leg aids. The reason his owner had thought he was dull and unresponsive was because she had never recognized his first impulse and had instead gone to battle with him over his refusal to go forward. Over time he had become more and more resentful of the legs and more sulled up when asked to go forward. And the thing is, at that point the request—i.e. to go forward—had been lost in the battle over going forward. He was *resisting the insistence* to go forward, while the thing being insisted upon (going forward) had become lost in the dust of the skirmish.

I found him to be more adversely reactive to my right leg than my left, but it only took a whisper of leg pressure for him to resist strongly. He had come to associate leg aids with being harshly booted, spurred or whipped, so his first impulse was a reaction to what he anticipated would follow. However, he **was** reacting to my leg aids (albeit the wrong reaction) and he was reacting to an extremely light pressure, so that's the point where I stayed and worked through it— i.e. at that initial reaction to my very light request. After that first ride when I realized how defensive he was about the leg aids, I spent a few sessions with him on the lunge line teaching him to trot and canter from verbal cues. When he understood the verbal cues and readily responded to them, I rode him again. The next time I rode him I applied a hint of leg aid, which caused him to pin his ears and prepare himself to go to battle with me by sulling up, but I never applied more leg pressure than that very small amount. Instead, I maintained that light leg and added the verbal cue to trot. At first, he didn't pay attention to my verbal cue, he was too focused on what he thought would be the usual ensuing battle, but after a moment he realized my leg was not getting stronger, and I was not going to battle with him. At that point, he also began to hear my verbal cue and he realized *"Hey, I know what that means!"* After thinking about that for a minute, he trotted off. When he trotted off I immediately removed my leg aid completely and I verbally praised him as I stroked his neck.

Once he learned I wasn't going to fight with him, he became more and more responsive to my leg aids and I was able to phase out the verbal cues. But during this process I had a big responsibility: I could not jeopardize his trust by using strong leg aids and/or fighting with him when he didn't respond immediately. I had to go through the process and wait for him to realize again and again and again that it wasn't going to become a battle. And each time he did go forward as his first impulse, I praised him lavishly. But those times he slipped back into his old routine and began to sull up as his first impulse, that's where I stayed. If his first impulse was not what I wanted, then I stayed with that first impulse, and with my super light request, until he complied. Even if we had done more advanced work in a prior ride, if he slipped back in his responses, then we dealt with that issue and not the work he was capable of doing. Eventually he became a horse that responded to extremely light leg aids. It was his preference that the leg aids be extremely light, and what I did was respect that preference. I personally like to use a slightly firmer leg aid than he liked, but with him I used a whisper of a leg. I believe horses should have a say in how we ride them, and light leg aids was important to him.

Another concept that goes along with training the first impulse is the one I think of as *training for tomorrow*. What I mean by this is when I work with a horse, my focus is never on how much I can get done that day; instead I'm thinking *"How is what I do today going to affect the way this horse comes back and works for me tomorrow?"* And that concept can be drawn out into *"How is what I do this week going to affect the way he works next week?"* And..."*How is what I do this year going to affect the way he works next year?"* And finally..."*How is what I do when he's young going to affect the way he is when he's old?"* It's very easy to get caught up in a good work session and milk it for all it's worth. I call that getting greedy, but that's apt to leave the horse feeling exploited and less than generous the next time we work with him. How can he give us anything if we never stop taking? As an example, say you had a handful of dollar bills and you planned on giving me one or two of them, but as soon as I saw them I began snatching them out of your hand. You would not be able to willingly give me a dollar, and my actions would probably cause you to clutch them tightly so I couldn't take anymore. Horses become the same way. We need to allow them the chance to be generous.

Some horses with truly charitable natures will work their hardest despite demanding riders, but others can turn sour in their work and become stingy in their efforts, or retreat within themselves.

When the temptation arises to drill on something repeatedly, it's good to ask yourself how that monotonous repetition will affect the way the horse will come back and work for you tomorrow? Excessive repetitions often simply turn horses into mindless robots. Do we want a partner who is a mindless robot? Or do we want a partner who is willingly interactive and remains a lively companion? Some riders purposely try to squelch a horse's energy because they are afraid of it, but a horse's strength and energy are only frightening if the horse uses them against us. If he uses his strength and agility for us, there is nothing to fear. We need to focus on showing him how to work with us, and use his power to our advantage instead of trying to diminish his power because it might get out of hand. In fact, it is often our focus on restraining a horse's energy or preventing him from using it that causes him to become defensive, and when defensive he will be far more likely to use himself against us, which is the Catch-22.

Power Over Fear

Fear is a huge issue with horses and one of the primary things we need to do is help them overcome their fears. Some horse owners seem to think the way to do that is to show a horse he is powerless to his fear/s. I've seen people tie horses up and then sack them out in such a way that it should be called freak them out because the horses are terrified, but they are tied up so they can't escape. There is a certain amount of resignation that goes along with feeling powerless to something, and some times the human thinks that resignation signifies that the horse has accepted his fate or that he's all right with the situation. But resignation is not acceptance; it's giving up, and it has a fatalistic element to it. It is a form of submission, but it results in a win/lose situation. Rather than making a horse feel powerless to his fear/s, we need to show him he has power over his fear/s—then we have a win/win. We win because the horse is no longer afraid, and he wins because he has conquered his fear.

Most horses instinctively associate fear with flight—i.e. they instinctively run from their fears because their survival depends on not being caught or trapped. So the first step in giving them power over their fear is to show them they are not being chased, then allow them to move if they feel the need, and finally show them that they can be the pursuers. For example, I use a tarp as one item to give a horse power over his fear. Where I start depends on the degree of fear of the tarp, but let's say the fear level is high. In that case, I start with a horse turned loose in a large enclosed area, like an arena. A round pen might be too small for a horse who is very afraid of a tarp. I tie a string onto the tarp so I can slowly drag it across the dirt. The horse will likely be afraid of it as it moves, and he will look for a way to escape out of the arena, so my goal is to make sure I don't drag the tarp closer to the horse. No matter which way he runs, I will drag the tarp away from him. Eventually he will realize that the tarp is not getting closer to him and his attention will shift from looking for an escape route to actually looking at the tarp. If he looks at the tarp, even for an instant, I will stop dragging it. I want him to realize that he has the power to make the tarp stop moving by focusing his attention on it. This is a key element in the process.

I might have to stop dragging the tarp several times for him to realize that when he stops and looks at the tarp, then it stops moving. Once he realizes that he is the one that is making the tarp stop moving, his curiosity will begin to replace his fear. When he is reasonably content to stand and watch the tarp (vs. try to run from it) then I will begin to slowly drag the tarp directly away from him. This next step is designed to encourage him to pursue the tarp. I want to turn the tables for him and show him that he is able to be the pursuer instead of the pursued. I want him to think he has the power to chase the tarp away. In that way, he will begin to develop power over his fear of the tarp instead of feeling powerless to it.

Once a horse begins to feel power over his fear, he may show signs of aggression toward it. This relates back to the pendulum swing, so if his fear of the tarp was great and he felt a strong urge to run away from it, then once his fear subsides his behavior might swing the other way and he might become aggressive toward the tarp by pawing or biting at it. That's his way of saying to the tarp *"Take that, you stupid tarp. You don't scare me!"* Usually that aggressive tendency will subside as he becomes increasingly less fearful, but those aggressive actions also indicate that the fear is still just under the surface, so it's important not to do something to undermine his progress. I try to discourage the biting of things like a tarp or plastic bags because the horse can bite it as a means of showing the object it doesn't scare him, but he won't realize his teeth are clamped onto it and when he brings his head up, the tarp or plastic will be still be in his mouth and that could instantly turn his curiosity back into full blown fear.

By systematically setting up situations in which we can show the horse he has power over his fear, we can begin turning his fear into curiosity, and it is through curiosity that he overcomes his fear. I once heard someone say curiosity is the flip side of fear in a horse, and

I think that's right. When the horse is comfortable touching the tarp on the ground and even walking on it, then we can pick it up and allow him to sniff it. From there it can actually touch his body (neck or shoulder initially), and as long as he's all right with that, we can begin to desensitize him to the tarp touching him all over. I do this work with either the horse at liberty or on a long line so he can move away from the tarp if he needs to. I do not prevent a horse's escape for desensitization work. The goal is not to show him he can't get away, but rather to show him he doesn't need to, and we show him he doesn't need to get away by allowing him to get away, as ironic as that sounds. He might run off from it any number of times, but each time he realizes the tarp is not chasing him and not hurting him, he will begin to realize he doesn't need to run from it, so even though he runs off, if there is no bad consequence, he'll come back to it. Horses assess the validity of a fear by the outcome. If a horse is afraid of something and then experiences pain, his fear is validated. But if he is afraid and nothing bad happens, his fear begins to subside and curiosity will take over.

    I remember a horse I bought a number of years ago who was very timid and fearful of people. Shortly after I bought him it was the middle of summer and the horseflies were out in droves. They bothered the horses worse at dusk, and all my horses would run up to the barn at dusk so I could go out and kill the horseflies that were swarming around them. They all knew the drill—I would wait until a horsefly landed on their body and then give it a solid hit with my hand to kill it, or at least stun it so I could step on it when it fell to the ground. If you've ever killed a horsefly you know it takes a rather hard hit.

    I'd never done that to this timid gelding, but he came up to the barn with the other horses one evening. I went from horse to horse killing the horseflies, and then one was buzzing around this gelding. I stood beside him waiting for the fly to land, which it did on his rump, and I gave him a solid hit. Unfortunately I missed the horsefly, and the horse shot off as if from a cannon and ran down the hill about 300 feet away. He then turned around and looked at the other horses as if to say *"Get out of there! Don't you see she's hitting us?"* But the other horses didn't move for they knew I was ridding them of the horseflies. After a little bit the gelding slowly made his way back up to the rest of us. Again, a horsefly was buzzing around him, and again I tried to hit it; this time it was on his withers and again I missed. He was still afraid of me hitting him and he ran off again, though not as far and not as fast. Then he turned around to watch what was going on and I could see the wheels turning in his head as he tried to figure it all out.

Finally he approached the group, and again a horsefly buzzed around his body and landed on his back. I tried to make it very clear to him that I was trying to hit the horsefly and not him personally, so I hovered my hand over the horsefly in an obvious manner. That time I hit the horsefly and killed it, but the most important part of that interaction was that the horse *got it*. He understood that I was trying to kill the horsefly and not hurt him. That understanding was a pivotal turning point in my relationship with him. From then on he understood that I could do things that would normally cause him fear, but there was probably a reason I was doing them and he was willing to find out what the reason was. He had taken power over his own fear, and his fears steadily decreased from that point onward.

Teaching a timid horse to be a pursuer can greatly increase his confidence level, and we can teach him to pursue any number of objects, like a tarp, a plastic bag tied onto a string, a beach ball, a rolling barrel, or anything he's afraid of. I've ridden a number of young horses who are afraid of machinery, like tractors pulling harrows or manure spreaders, and one of the best ways to get them over that fear is ride them up behind the tractor as it goes away from them. If someone brings the tractor with the water tank or harrow into the arena as I'm riding, I'll have the horse follow along behind it as it makes its rounds. The horse begins to feel that he's chasing the big, noisy thing away from him and his fear of it subsides. In addition, taking power over one fear will have a carry-over effect to other fears. Each fear that is overcome causes the horse to be braver the next time he's faced with a fear and his overall confidence will begin to snowball.

There are any number of things horses are afraid of and we often need to get creative to figure out ways to give him power over those fears, but the more empowered he feels, the less fearful he will be in general. Some people will say *"That's all well and good to let him chase things away, but what happens when I'm riding out in the field and a plastic bag blows toward him and I can't control the situation and make the bag go away?"* Good question. In our desensitization work we will first show the horse he can be the pursuer, and being the pursuer changes the outcome of the experience for him. Remember that horses determine whether or not a fear is valid by the outcome, so if he's afraid of a tarp, or a plastic bag, or a barrel, or whatever it is, and he can turn the tables on that fear, the outcome will empower him. Since horses tend to generalize information, he will eventually begin to feel empowered over a variety of fears. Once he feels empowered over the tarp in terms of knowing he can chase it away, he will be much more receptive to the tarp touching him and then even coming toward him. And once he is accepting of a tarp coming toward him, he will begin to generalize that information and he'll be more accepting of a plastic bag or a ball or a wild turkey, etc. coming toward him as well. It won't happen overnight, but with a consistently positive outcome, it will happen, and even before he gets to where he's totally all right with scary things, he'll become *enough* all right with them that they won't scare the daylights out of him.

The flip side of this situation is the horse who is punished for reacting to his fear so he learns to internalize the fear. That's an example of a horse who has been trained to be a *hunkered down rabbit* [6]. You may think that horse isn't afraid because he stands still, but he can be withholding a good deal of fear inside. That withheld fear can turn him into a lit stick of dynamite and the only question is how long is the fuse? That horse feels powerless to his fear, so he swallows it and holds it in as long as he can. But when something happens and he can't hold it in any longer, he'll explode leaving the human scratching his head wondering *"Where the heck did that come from?"* But if we'll go through the process of giving a horse power over his fear/s, he may show some strong fear reactions initially, but at least we'll know he's afraid and we won't be fooled into thinking everything's fine when it's not.

Anxiety/Tension and Release

I use the word *anxiety* to refer to a general state of being—i.e. a state of inner turmoil which can have a variety of causes—and *tension* as the physical manifestation of anxiety. The two go together. A horse's inner state of being is associated with his emotions. There is a wide range of emotions horses are capable of feeling, and each emotion will elicit certain behaviors although those behaviors may vary with each horse. One horse may bolt from fear while another one will shut down and become rooted to the spot, but it is important to be aware of the emotions horses can feel and to know that very often the horse's behavior/s are a reflection of his emotional or inner state. I use the term anxiety as a catch-all phrase to refer to any sort of inner turmoil which results in tension. The most common causes of anxiety are:

- Fear
- Pain
- Confusion
- Resentment

Other emotions that cause anxiety and adversely affect behavior are:

- Frustration
- Annoyance
- Depression
- Apathy
- Grief
- Rage

- Sadness
- Worry

Tension (physical) and anxiety (emotional) can have different causes, but they are two of the biggest problems I see in horses today, and many times their owners are not even aware of the degree to which their horses are tense, anxious, and/or afraid. I have talked with owners who think the undesired behaviors of their horses are normal equine behaviors, yet I would attribute many of those behaviors to tension and/or anxiety. The overtly obvious behaviors that result from emotional turmoil are things such as bolting, spooking, rearing, biting, and kicking, but other behaviors that aren't as obviously caused by inner anxiety are things such as not standing still, being constantly distracted, calling to other horses, invading your space, etc. Those things are often considered straight forward training issues, yet they will most likely disappear or diminish if or when the horse becomes calm inside. You can also see the signs of tension or anxiety in the way a horse moves. He will not have a fluid, rhythmic movement, even though he might move quickly or even with agility. Very quick movement is often a horse's attempt to get out of the way of the human, and in that context it is defensive and arises from anxiety. Some owners think if their horse is not doing something overtly unsettling, like bucking, rearing, bolting, spooking, etc., then the horse must be relaxed, and yet many horses have learned to internalize their anxiety so they do not clearly convey it. A horse can appear calm in his actions but still be an internal cauldron of emotion, so we can't simply look at his outward behavior to determine whether or not he is calm on the inside. We need to learn to see the telltale signs that indicate inner turmoil before it escalates to an obvious outward expression, otherwise the horse becomes a ticking time bomb. Those signs will be evident in his eyes, ears, lips, tail and general body language.

If a horse is prone to fear we can give him power over his fear and encourage him to calm his anxiety, but we also need to pay attention to the things he does as he releases his fear and/or anxiety so we can specifically reward that release. We want him to know that his inner calm and physical relaxation are the first and foremost goals of our training. They are the first rung of the training ladder. I visualize two vertical bars, as on a graph, in regard to training. One bar is performance—i.e. all the things the horse learns how to do—and the other bar is anxiety. Often times the two bars rise together as a horse's training progresses, but we want the anxiety bar to remain low as the training bar increases. I think it is safe to assume that any horse will experience a degree of anxiety when first being handled by humans, so from the very first encounters we need to be trying to alleviate any doubts, apprehensions, or fears the horse might be feeling.

We can't guarantee we will never cause a horse to feel anxious, but we can show him how to release his anxiety. If he doesn't learn how to release he will perform while withholding anxiety which can vary from slight to great. Everything he learns to do in terms of performance he will learn to do in a state of tension and withheld anxiety. That tension will not only hinder his physical efforts, it will also make him more prone to injury, and can even lead to an earlier onset of arthritic conditions. Tension is withheld in the muscles, so they will be in a constant state of contraction which makes them less flexible. If he extends a limb and it impacts the ground far in front of his body the ground will hold the foot in place, and if the muscles don't have the sufficient ability to lengthen in that extended position then the effort will pull a tendon or a ligament. Tight muscles are stronger than tendons or ligaments, but it is tendon or ligament damage that can end or diminish performance careers. A horse's system is designed for amazing physical efforts, but it is crucial we show him how to operate in a state of calmness and free from tension.

The releases of tension or anxiety will vary depending on the type of tension being felt. Often times the release of anxiety or tension will result in the horse:

- softly blowing out his nostrils
- lightly shaking his head/neck
- sighing
- making a licking or chewing motion with his mouth
- passing gas
- groaning

Blowing out the nostrils is a common sign, and I like to hear that, or some other sign of release, as part of every warm-up routine. The soft nostril blowing that indicates release of tension is not to be confused with the quicker, harder snorts out the nostrils that indicate the horse is alarmed or overly fresh. A horse can let out a deep groan as a release, but that is sometimes associated with either a physical discomfort or a deep-seated, almost visceral, release.

Since calmness and relaxation are so important in horse training I find it beneficial to specifically reward the releases of tension/anxiety when they occur. If a horse is very tight or tense then releasing is my primary training goal and I will praise any sign of release of tension. I want the horse to understand that getting to a place of emotional calm and physical relaxation within himself is the goal, and that goal is never abandoned as the training progresses. The calm we want is in the horse's mind, and the relaxation we want is the release of the horse's long back muscles—his topline. I find showing a horse how to release is ultimately more important, and more practical, than trying to never create anxiety in the first place. I see some riders tiptoe around their nervous horses so as not to upset them further, but that actually often adds to the horse's anxiety. He can feel that something is amiss but he doesn't realize it is his rider's worry about HIM. We need to combat a horse's anxiety by being calm and confident within ourselves, and tip-toeing is not done from a place of calm confidence. The horse picks up on the fact that the person is anxious even if the person thinks he's acting quietly.

One of the visual images I use in training is of the trick performers who spin plates on the tops of poles. I used to see them on late night television shows. They will start a plate spinning on a pole, then add another, and another, etc. Periodically the earlier plates will begin to wobble and the performer needs to go back and get the plate spinning again. It wouldn't be much of a trick if they got plate #6 spinning while plates #1 and 2 fell off and broke. So I think of our training goals as those plates, and the first plate is calmness, relaxation, and attentiveness. Anytime that first plate begins to wobble I go back and re-establish it before proceeding. To me it's not much of a training feat if my horse can perform canter half-pass, or slide to a stop, or jump a big fence, but he is anxious, tense and distracted as he does it.

Another analogy I think of is a computer's operating system. The early computers operated in DOS, which I understand was complicated and difficult to learn. Then the PC's came out with Windows, which was more user-friendly, but whatever the operating system is, all the programs on the computer operate within that system. Horses also have an operating system. Some of them operate from a place of calmness, trust, confidence, and willingness; some from a place of frustration or resentment; while others operate from a place of fear or intimidation. The latter perform because they are afraid not to. Everything a horse learns to do he learns to do within the context of his operating system. A computer has programs loaded onto it, and a horse's programs are the repertoire of performance maneuvers he has learned. If a horse is trained through intimidation, he will not only operate in a state of tension/anxiety, but everything he learns will be learned within the context of that tension/anxiety, which will affect him physically as well as mentally and emotionally. Re-training that horse is not simply a matter of focusing on his performance, in severe cases it involves taking off all the *programs*, re-configuring the operating system, and then re-loading the programs.

Horses use muscles to perform physical movements, but the muscles used in performance vary based on the internal state of being. A horse will use different muscles and/or use muscles differently if he performs in a state of anxiety vs. a state of relaxation. So while we first need to change his internal state of being we also need to allow him to relearn the movements within the new state of being. Some horses are so tense in their work that when you get them to a state of relaxation they have lost much of their conditioning; the muscles that were conditioned were the muscles associated with anxiety (which is often associated with *flight mode* in a horse). It will require a different usage of muscles to perform the same movements in a state of relaxation, and in many ways the process is similar to starting a young horse from scratch.

If I were granted one wish and could change one thing in the lives of horses today it would be to eliminate the tension and anxiety felt by many domesticated horses around the world.

I see tension and anxiety as perhaps the biggest problem in modern day horses which results in mental, emotional and physical repercussions. Many of the early onset physical problems that end or diminish equine careers—things like arthritis, or strained tendons/ligaments, etc.—are very often caused by work done in a state of tension and anxiety. Fortunately there are many people who recognize this and are taking appropriate measures to ensure calmness and relaxation in their horses, but there are many who are not.

Mind to Feet Connection

When dealing with horses, there are many things that fall under the heading of *reciprocal relationships*. One of the most well known reciprocal relationships is the one between mind and body. They are so intertwined it becomes difficult to determine which one is the cause and which one is the effect. If you carry that thought further it means you can gain one thing through the other. For example, a primary theme of my books is how a horse's emotional or inner state can dictate his behaviors, meaning there is a reciprocal relationship between emotion and behavior. If a horse is feeling fear, he will act afraid—he will want to escape; if he's feeling frustrated, he will act frustrated—he might paw, or shake his head/neck vigorously; if he's feeling resentful, he will act resentful—he will pin his ears and maybe swish his tail to display his resentment, and he might even become aggressive. So if we want to change his behaviors—the desire to flee, the pawing and head shaking, the ear pinning, etc.—we need to alleviate the emotions or underlying feelings that fuel those behaviors. If we only try to squelch the behavior/s, we may be successful, but the horse will still be feeling the emotion that initially caused the behavior. If he is trained through intimidation he can be made to be afraid to act on his emotions, but they still exist and the behavioral problems they cause will always be right under the surface. Suffice it to say there exists a reciprocal relationship between mind and body, and between emotion and behavior, as well as numerous other reciprocal relationships. But the one I will discuss in this chapter is the one between the mind and the feet.

The horse's physical body is comprised of two skeletons, the axial skeleton (the spine) and the appendicular skeleton (the legs). Our riding goal is to be able to utilize the horse's whole body at our will, but to gain that cooperation from him we need to understand more about his body, his mind, and how they most naturally interact with one another. What we have the most obvious feeling of when we ride a horse is his body, his mass, or more specifically, his axial skeletal system (his spine from head to tail including his ribcage). Each skeleton has its own musculature, and when you look at the axial skeletal system as a whole, it comprises the bulk of the animal. His appendicular skeleton (his legs) is much less weighty in terms of mass, and yet it is through that skeleton (specifically the feet) that we are best able to influence the animal as a whole.

I don't believe horses have a clear conscious understanding of how their spine/body operates. I think their body merely goes along for the ride, so to speak, that is dictated by their thoughts or emotional state and carried out by their feet. So when we ride them and we try to influence their body (their posture), our requests aren't always readily understood by them. This can cause resistance, and since it is their mass we are trying to change, they resist with their mass which is the bulk and the strength of their body. Hence, we resort to stronger bits, more gadgets, longer spurs, etc. to try to overcome the resistance of their mass/weight.

Horses readily understand how their feet move. We can easily teach them to move their feet forward, sideways, or backward, and we can isolate the movement of one foot at a time. Through being able to move the feet wherever we want, we gain access to the animal as a whole. If we can readily and fluidly send the feet either forward, backward, or sideways at will, we have control over the animal. I teach horses from the ground to move a foot by first applying a light feel to the halter rope. If the foot that I want to move doesn't move, I will touch the leg with the end of a whip (not whack it, but simply touch it). If the touch is very light, like a fly, the horse will most likely pick up the foot/leg which is a reaction that can be rewarded. Yet I see people try to move their horse by leaning up against them and pushing against their body. A horse's instinctive reaction to his body being pushed will be to plant his feet and brace his body because he feels he is being pushed off balance. So he's planting the very things we want to move, i.e. his feet.

Aside from gaining access to the horse's whole body, teaching him how and where to move his feet has another distinct advantage which is that he associates the moving of feet with dominance. For example, a submissive horse will move his feet out of the way of a dominant horse. You've likely seen a dominant horse in the pasture walk toward a pile of hay or the water trough, and any less dominant horses will move out of his way. It is their feet they are moving, so if we can teach the horse to move his feet out of our space he will automatically respect our dominance, and we don't have to hurt him or scare him or beat him up to do that. We simply teach him how to move his feet at our request, and then move them out of *our* space.

Have you ever seen a horse who, when you walk up to him, will raise his head and move his head out of your way but will not move his feet? That horse is not submissive, and he would never do that to a dominant horse. If we walk toward a horse assertively we want him to move his feet out of our way, and by moving his feet, he has to move his whole body. By standing his ground and moving only his head/neck, he's saying *"Yeah, whatever. I guess I can move my head, but you don't command enough respect for me to move my feet for you."* Another theme on this type of disrespect is the horse who stands close to the human and swings his head back and forth looking at things while his handler ducks so as not to get hit. That horse is not necessarily being belligerent or mean, but he is being disrespectful. He needs to be shown how to move his feet a respectful distance away from the human.

On the other hand, many horses can get *stuck* in their feet, and that can be due to a variety of reasons, like fear, tension, anxiety, confusion, etc. Those are the horses who have learned to internalize their emotions so they are afraid to move for fear of making a mistake. They feel like their feet have grown roots and are literally planted into the ground. Their movement is definitely not free and fluid. We want a horse to readily move his feet (first response) and then we can direct where they go (second response). But if we punish him because he moved his feet in the wrong direction, even though he did move them, he may end up simply getting stuck in his feet to avoid the punishment. That's a classic example of squelching a horse's *try*.

Other horses can be perpetual motion machines—they want to move their feet all the time. Again, that's likely due to inner anxiety as well, but it's an externalized version of it. With the horse who moves too much, instead of punishing his movement we can say to him *"Great idea to trot off like that-! How about trotting a circle the size of a dinner plate?"* And when he says *"I think I've had enough of that, I'd rather walk"*, we can say *"Another great idea-!"* That way he'll end up walking, which is what we wanted him to do in the first place, but in the process we have actually lessened, rather than increased, his internal anxiety. After a while, he'll become calmer overall, he will realize he doesn't need to get away, and he will be more willing to walk or stop when we ask.

Some riding disciplines (like dressage training) are largely concerned with the posture of the horse (i.e. the way he carries and uses his spine), and there also exists a reciprocal relationship between the placement of the footfalls and posture. A horse will use his feet one way when he's traveling *hollow* in his back, and he'll use his feet another when he's released and traveling *through* his back (or what some call *round*). This means his feet will support a particular posture, whether that posture is the one we want or not. But it also means that we can show him how to utilize his feet to support the posture we do want.

One of the first things I teach a horse is how to position his feet to support a bend in his spine. Bend is a fundamental ingredient in developing a horse for riding. All horses are naturally crooked, and a horse can never truly be straight if he is unable to bend equally in both directions. A horse can be quick and he can be agile, but he cannot be supple without the ability to equally bend to both sides. Bend occurs between the withers and the croup, and while the back does not have the ability to bend evenly or to a great degree, it does have some bending capability. The bend in the ribcage is accompanied by axial rotation, which means the ribcage rotates like a big barrel. In a left bend, the ribcage rotates so the withers go right and the sternum goes left. In other words, the bottom of the ribcage rotates inward to the inside of a bend. This is important to note as many riders will attempt to encourage bend by using a strong inside leg aid, which actually pushes the bottom of the ribcage outward. Bend is not to be confused with what occurs in the neck. Granted, the bend in the neck should match the bend in the back, but the neck is able to bend to a greater degree than the back. There is no gymnastic benefit to bending the neck more than the rest of the spine, yet an over bent neck is commonly seen. Once a horse learns to over bend his neck he can use that to actually disconnect from the rest of his spine. When I was young we called that a *rubber neck*.

The inside hind leg will step toward the midline of the body (which is aligned over the line of travel) to support a bend. In a left bend, the left hind steps toward the right (or the midline) in order to be under the horse's center of gravity. That will allow him to freely move his front feet around the turn or circle. The opposite will apply to a right bend. Those particular steps can be taught from the ground or the saddle through turns on forehand. [7] When a horse is resistant to bend it is very often due to an issue of footfalls. All horses are inherently crooked, and they will weight one front foot more than the other. A horse who weights his right front foot more than the left will be reluctant to bend to the right. He will need to learn to shift some of the weight over to his left front. Turns around the haunches are a good way to teach him how to move his front feet left or right. Being able to step under his center of gravity equally with either hind foot and then equalizing the weight between his front feet will enable a horse to bend.

When a horse is defensive he will want to adopt a stance that will best prepare him for possible flight, and that stance will cause him to want to carry his hind feet back behind his body because that's the position from which they can most effectively push or propel him forward. That stance will cause him to be tight in his back because it is easier to propel a tight back than a relaxed one; an example would be trying to propel a stick vs. a piece of rope. If he's spooky, he will likely want to keep his front feet in a wider stance so he can quickly push off one or the other front foot to wheel or spin away from something. So the stance of his feet is widened and/or lengthened to support a defensive posture. That means that to support a posture more suitable to our needs, we want to show him how to shorten and narrow his base of support by engaging his pelvis, or flexing his lumbo-sacral joint, which will bring his hind feet more under his mass vs. out behind him. We can use movements such as shoulder-in and haunches-in to increase engagement and enhance posture. So we can address the issue of posture via the placement of his feet, and the biggest advantage of doing it that way is most horses readily understand foot placement.

The Rein Aids

In order to take a horse out of flight mode you can first teach him to place his feet the opposite of how he would place them in flight mode. I begin from the ground, but eventually want to be able to place the feet while riding, and for that I need to teach the horse certain rein aids. There is more than one set of rein aids that instructors teach students. The first set is the one I learned in Pony Club and it included the opening and leading rein, the direct rein, the indirect rein, the counter (or bearing) rein, and the pulley rein (for the strong horse). There is another set of rein aids employed by the German method of dressage training (as described in *The Principles of Riding—The Official Instruction Handbook of the German National Equestrian Federation*). They are:

- The *regulating rein* (used in conjunction with the weight and leg aids)
- The *yielding rein* (self-explanatory—also used to encourage the horse to lengthen his neck and topline)
- The *supporting rein* (used on the outside to support the turn and control the degree of bend)
- The *non-allowing rein* (used with the forward driving aids until the horse becomes light in the hand)

If you think of these rein aids in terms of the horse's two skeletal systems, this set of rein aids *speaks* primarily to the horse's spine or body/mass, with the intention of altering his posture. But the rein aids I prefer to use are the ones described by Jean Froissard in *Classical Horsemanship for Our Time*. That set of rein aids *speaks* to the horse's feet. They are:

- The *opening rein* (which moves the corresponding front foot toward the rein aid)
- The *counter rein* (which moves the corresponding front foot away from the rein aid)
- The *direct rein of opposition* (which moves the corresponding hind foot away from the rein aid)
- The *counter rein of opposition passing behind the withers* (which moves both front and hind feet away from the rein aid—rather like a leg yield)
- The (right) *counter rein of opposition in front of the withers* (which moves the front feet to the left and the hind feet to the right)

Don't let the complex names discourage you. The actions of these aids are very distinct even if you can't remember their names. I generally use and teach the first 3 rein aids. It seems to me the 4th is basically a combined effect of the counter rein and the direct rein of opposition. One of the complaints of the German method of training is that it can cause the horse to become heavy in the hand, and while I don't believe that occurs so much when the method is employed by a tactful, educated rider, I do believe there is an inherent risk of heaviness because the rein aids seem to address more the mass or weight of the horse. The French rein aids, since they address the footfalls, should *bypass* (if you will) the resistance of the horse's mass. I think of the French rein aids like putting a key into a keyhole, i.e. if the key is lined up accurately with the hole, you can insert it easily and unlock the door. When using the rein aids, if the position or influence of the rein aid is precise, the feet will readily move. For that reason, the French rein aids are more about precision than strength.

There exists a palpable response in which the feet just glide to or away from the rein aid if the aid is precise, and the rider remains centered and balanced when giving it. Using the rein aid/s with more strength is actually counter-productive. Many riders sacrifice the tactfulness of their rein aids by holding them too long and/or shifting their weight in a counter-productive way in order to give more strength to the rein aid/s.

*Since the rein aids move the feet it is paramount
they be given in time with the footfalls,
meaning they are given and released very quickly.*

The German rein aids are dependent upon the accuracy and sophistication of the leg and seat aids in conjunction with the rein aids, which means the rider who does not yet possess an independent, supple seat stands a greater chance of triggering resistance in the horse utilizing those rein aids. I personally find horses and novice riders both progress more easily using the French rein aids. I have noticed over the years a distinct unconscious correlation in riders between their hands and their seats in that their seats tend to do what their hands are doing. Meaning, if they yield their hands forward, they will lose their seat and their lower back will become wobbly. Conversely, if they tighten their hands/arms, their seat will become fixed and rigid. An independent, supple seat is one that follows (or influences) the horse's back regardless of what the hands or legs are doing. The aids—hands, legs, seat, upper body, and weight—all work in harmony with one another but independently.

It is a traditional belief that one must develop an independent seat before utilizing any rein aids, which is a good approach because one of the best ways to develop the seat is to let go of the controlling tendency of the hands/arms. Letting go of the arms causes the seat and upper body to become balanced and independent because there is not the false sense of security one feels when clutching with the hands/arms. One misunderstood concept I see in riders is the notion of a *consistent contact* with the bit. Too many riders simply lock their arms (and consequently their seats) in attempt to maintain a consistent contact, and yet true contact is dependent upon the ability to yield and/or follow the horse's mouth. Many riders mistakenly employ a rigid hand and call it consistent contact.

A young horse often loses his balance when first started under saddle, and when that happens his instinct is to utilize his head and neck to regain it. If his rider is truly maintaining a light, consistent contact with his mouth, the rider will yield his hands to accommodate those balancing motions the horse makes with his head and neck. Over time, the horse's balance and carriage will become steadier and he will become able to maintain a consistent head and neck position, and when that happens, the rider will be able to maintain a consistent hand position. Yet many riders simply fix their hands in a certain position before the horse has stabilized his balance and they call that a consistent contact, but in actuality, that kind of contact will vary from light to very strong depending on the horse's balance, and obviously there is nothing consistent about a varying contact. The key to maintaining a consistent contact lies in the rider's ability to disconnect, if you will, their arms from the balance and stability of their seat and upper body in order to follow the horse's mouth. Many riders, when yielding the hands forward, will let their upper bodies fall forward along with their hands, which in turn pulls them *out of their seat*. The hands (and arms) need to be able to yield forward with no change in the upper body balance or seat stability.

Since the French rein aids are given to direct the feet, there is only a small window of opportunity in which that can be done. Every footfall of every stride contains 2 phases:

- a stance phase, and
- a flight phase.

The stance phase occurs when the foot is on the ground and the weight of the body is passing over it. The flight phase occurs when the foot is lifted as it moves through the air. The only time the placement of a footfall can be changed is when the foot is in the air as you obviously can't change the location of a grounded foot. Conversely, when slowing or stopping the feet the aid should be given as the foot/feet are coming to the ground and momentarily eased when they leave the ground again (until the horse either slows or stops). So the French rein aids need to be given as the foot is leaving the ground (for turning) or coming to the ground (for slowing or stopping) and then released when the foot enters the next phase. The biggest problem I see with riders giving rein aids is they hold the aid too long. Even a fraction of a second can be too long if it is not in time with appropriate phase of the footfalls. Once the rein aid disconnects from the footfall the horse will either resist or evade the aid, and the resistance or evasion will occur in his posture. A resistant horse will tighten his jaw, poll and back if a turning rein aid is held too long and he's unable to comply, while an evasive horse will curl his neck and escape the aid all together. I visualize the reins connecting to the feet like the strings on a marionette, and they *pick up and place* or *stop* each footfall in the rhythmic timing of the particular gait. This action alone requires the rider to be able to utilize his hands separately from his seat and in time with the horse's footfalls. When the training progresses those rein aids can be delivered as nothing more than little *energy impulses* which are directed by the seat and received by the hand.

It would seem logical to think if the reins are slack or loose, then the rider's hands/arms are independent from his seat, but that is not always the case. I see many riders tighten their shoulders, or clamp their underarm/s, or lock their elbow/s or wrist/s even when the reins are long and slack. The horse will feel that tightness through the rider's hips/seat, and he will often respond in a diminished manner, meaning the rider's tight seat will tend to decrease the horse's athletic efforts despite the long rein. Some horses will get faster from a tight seat and that may tie in with a perception on the horse's part of a predator on his back. But either way, locked hips disconnect from the horse's motion and the horse will react adversely unless or until he becomes so dull to the seat that he doesn't react at all. An independent, supple seat is one which follows the motions of the horse's back regardless of what the rest of the rider's body is doing. One of the best ways to achieve such a seat is to relinquish the controlling instinct of the hands and arms (which originates in the mind). The rider also needs to separate the actions of his arms from his upper body and seat for only then can any kind of rein aid be given effectively. The aids are given separately yet in harmony with one another.

The timing of the rein aids can be seen as well as felt more easily from the ground, as in lunging the horse or doing some ground work. To learn the timing you can lunge the horse and pick one particular foot to focus on, say the inside front foot. Then every time the inside front foot begins to come off the ground you can verbally say *now..now..now*...in time with that one footfall. Once you have the timing verbalized, you can add a light squeeze on the lunge line, as if you were giving a rein aid, to correlate with that timing. You want to keep that one foot stepping around the circle, which means it needs to step just a little bit to the inside on every step to continue on a curved line. Once your hand is connected to the horse's foot through his natural timing, it is very easy to keep him coming around you on a circle. Many horses lunge by turning their heads to the outside of the circle as the handler keeps a strong hold on their head so they don't just take off. That is a good example of a feel that is not connected to the footfall/s. Instead that handler is trying to contain the horse's body/mass which further triggers his flight response.

I had a farrier who I always enjoyed visiting with when he came to trim my horses, and I remember in particular a conversation we had one day. He was talking about an auction, it seems like it was for the cavalry, where the horses were presented on a wooden stage or platform that had a big curtain. Each horse was first presented with the curtain all the way down as he was trotted across the platform, so the horse could only be heard and not seen. Then the curtain was raised to his ankles, and he was trotted back across the platform. Then the curtain was raised to his knees and hocks, then elbows and stifles. At that point the horses were purchased. I never knew if that was actually done somewhere, and I'm not sure I personally would buy a horse on that basis, but it was still an intriguing thought to me. So for months after that, I would look only at a horses' feet and legs as I worked them from the ground or on the lunge line.

Eventually I got to where I could tell what their body was doing by the way they moved and placed their feet, and I also found I could influence their posture through their footfalls. But the best part of it, for me, was in realizing how much easier it was for the horses to understand what I wanted when I addressed their footfalls. I didn't have to *fight* their mass, yet I could still influence it. Many times if horses feel we are pushing or pulling their bodies/mass, they will brace their feet in response. If we can free up the feet, and learn to place the feet where we desire without the resistance in the body, we can gain access to the whole horse.

The key to influencing footfalls is to understand how you want the feet to move, and then ask for that movement within the timing of the footfalls. If a rein or lunge line aid is given out of time, the horse will tend to brace his feet and resist with his mass, or evade the request. Feel and timing are key, though I find with many riders that the timing will sort itself out when they first simply get in sync with the rhythm of the gait. In other words, they may rhythmically give a turning aid when the foot is on the ground, but if they give and release the aid in a light manner and in a consistent rhythm the horse will learn to turn once his foot leaves the ground, and then after a while the optimal timing will develop. So I would say the first step in learning the timing of the footfalls is simply to connect to the rhythm of the gait. Once in the rhythm the precise timing will often sort itself out.

Primary & Secondary Aids

We ask horses to go forward, stop, and turn, etc. with *aids*. The natural means we have at our disposal for giving those aids are our hands, legs, seat, upper body, and weight, and some might include voice. The aids can be classified in two categories: primary aids and secondary aids. I define the primary aids as the ones I want the finished horse to respond to, so they should be light, polite, and elicit a clear response. The secondary aids are used to either:

· clarify the primary aid, or
· motivate the horse to respond to the primary aid.

When starting a young horse I give the primary aid/s as my first request, and even though the horse likely doesn't understand or recognize their meaning I still always ask the horse for something first with my primary aid/s. Then if he doesn't respond, or he gives the wrong response, I employ one or more secondary aid/s. I prefer not to simply use a stronger version of a primary aid as a secondary aid.

For example, say I want a horse to go from a walk to a trot: I want the finished horse to trot off when I slightly point my seat bones toward his front feet and give him a light squeeze with my calves, so that's the first thing I do. Because the horse is green, he doesn't understand what that means, so let's say he does nothing. I will then come in with a secondary aid, but I don't want my secondary aid to be simply a stronger seat and/or leg aid—those are my primary aids, and I want them to always stay light and polite. So I might cluck to him or use a verbal cue (particularly if he already knows verbal cues) in addition to my primary aids. If he still doesn't go forward, I might tap him with a whip as I cluck and use my seat and leg aids. In that way I have *layered* several aids, and as soon as he shows a forward response, I'll quit all of the aids (i.e. negative reinforcement). The next time I ask for a trot transition, I ask first with my primary aids (always polite), and again I will begin to layer the aids if he doesn't respond. Eventually he will begin to recognize what the primary aids mean and he'll begin to respond to them without the addition of the secondary aids.

One of the reasons I don't like to use stronger versions of my primary aids as secondary aids is because it is too easy to end up with primary aids that are too strong. For example, if a light, polite leg aid on a scale of 1 to 10 is a 3, and the horse doesn't respond to that 3 leg aid, it is easy to increase it, say to a 5, until he does respond. Then the next time you ask with a 3, but get no response, you will be more apt to go to a 5 leg aid again to get him to respond. It's very easy to gradually get into a habit of asking initially with the stronger aid, the strength that gets the response, and at that point your primary aid has increased to a 5. Then if the horse begins to tune out the 5 leg aid, you increase to a 6, 7 or even an 8, and after a while he's tuning out some very strong leg aids and it's taking stronger and stronger leg aids to get any response from him at all.

Talking about pressure can be confusing or misleading due to personal interpretation. I remember in particular one man and one woman I was teaching a number of years ago because they took consecutive lessons, so the differences in their aid giving were particularly obvious. The man was overly strong in his aids and the woman was overly passive. My objective was to get each of them to give aids that rated what I would call about a 3 on a scale of 1 to 10. I would tell the man to pretend his leg was a feather in order to get him to lighten up to a 3, while I told the woman to kick her horse hard enough to push the breath out of him to get her to give an aid her horse would even recognize. So even reading these words and thinking about aids on a scale of 1 to 10 I'm sure will be interpreted differently by different readers.

Some people think the aids can't be too light, but I think they can. Aids that are in the 1 to 2 range (by my definition and perception) are aids that are a whisper. Sometimes it's good to whisper. Often times *whispering* is more effective at gaining a horse's attention than *screaming*. However, aid giving in general is a means of communication, and I personally would find it very annoying to carry on all my communication with other humans in a whisper. I don't like people to scream at me, but I also would not want people to only whisper either. Conversation is best at a normal conversational level, and that's the principle I use when I'm communicating with a horse via the aids. I want the intensity of the aids to be light and polite yet clear and definite—and for me that is about a 3. Five is the cross-over line, meaning primary aids stronger than a 5 are beyond the normal conversational level and entering the range that is too *loud*. Primary aids that become too loud are usually counter-productive. The horse will tend to resist them, tune them out, or in some cases become resentful of them.

While I'm careful not to increase my primary aids, I will, if necessary, increase the pressure of my secondary aids. In doing that I may *raise my voice*, but I am still very cognizant of trying not to *scream*. Using the example of the walk to trot transition: Once I know the horse understands what I want, if he chooses to be sluggish in his response I would still ask with my polite primary aids, but I might increase the pressure of the whip as a way of saying *"Hey! Pay attention to my leg."* And with an older horse who definitely knows what is expected of him, I might use the whip to get an over-reaction, meaning if he doesn't respond to the primary aid/s to trot off smartly I might ask him to jump into a canter from the whip. Then the choice I'm giving him is to either trot off smartly from my polite aids, or jump forward into the canter from the whip. Using the secondary aids in this manner is what I think of as motivating the horse to respond to the primary aid/s, though I typically find horses need that kind of tuning up because they have learned they can ignore the primary aids. I would also point out that using a stronger secondary aid as a motivational aid is different than using increased pressure as a punishment. When I increase the intensity of my secondary aid/s it is not to punish the horse for being sluggish—it is to motivate him to be more responsive. The difference between the two is largely one of my own underlying intention, so I make sure I am always intending to motivate and not to punish. I also will cease all aids once the response is given, and that in itself is reinforcement rather than punishment.

Another caveat is in order here. I talked earlier about the horse's *first impulse*, and while most horses will readily go forward to pressure, some horses will sull up (or suck back) if pressured to go forward. For that reason, I only use a whip or strong driving aids to get an over-reaction if the horse's first impulse is not to sull up. Many riders feel if a horse sulls up they need to use the whip even more strongly, and while that *may* work it can also backfire. If the horse is truly committed to not going forward, for whatever reason, and you come in with a strong whip (or spur), he might rear up and possibly go over backwards. So I take into account the horse's first impulse before increasing the pressure of my secondary aids. If his first impulse is not the impulse I want, I change the impulse before coming in more firmly—either that or think up another tactic that doesn't trigger that wrong first impulse.

One example of the above would be the difference between a sluggish forward response vs. fear of going past an object (or reluctance to move due to pain, etc.). A sluggish forward response is still a forward response, so the increased pressure of the secondary aid will motivate the horse to respond more quickly. However if a horse is reluctant to move forward due to fear, say of an object that frightens him, then increasing the pressure to go forward will need to override his fear in order to succeed. And even if it does override his fear and he goes past the object, his fear has not necessarily been alleviated. So in that case I would look for an alternative tactic and not simply put more pressure on him to go forward.

While the secondary aids can motivate the horse to respond to the primary aid/s, they can also explain or clarify the primary aid/s. For example, if we're teaching the very green horse how to turn toward an opening or leading rein, he may wallow around if he doesn't understand the concept. Instead of simply pulling harder on the rein, we can add the secondary aid of a whip moving up and down beside his face (even more compelling with a small flag on the end). His natural inclination will be to move his head *away* from the waving whip, and when he does he will move *toward* the rein, which is the desired response. You can also use the small flag to draw his curiosity toward the rein aid, but either way we can then praise him and release both aids. After a few repetitions he will realize it's the moving toward the rein that is being praised and he'll begin to offer that without the secondary aid of the waving whip. In that way, the secondary aid *explained* to him what the primary aid meant.

I will also use things such as the wall as a secondary aid. I rode a gelding one time who was not a runaway, but he had no brakes. He would just run right through the rein aids with his jaw and poll locked. I wanted to get him to where he responded to a light rein aid even though he completely tuned it out. I started at the walk, and I walked him straight toward the wall. Before he reached it, I asked lightly with the reins for him to stop, but he continued on. So I just let him walk into the wall, at which point I praised him. He did stop after all; just because he had no choice was beside the point. I did that several times the first ride and he began to slow down from the light rein aid. The next ride he was stopping from the walk with a light rein aid, so I did the same thing at the trot. Before long he was listening to the rein aids and slowing or stopping nicely from a light feel. As is often the case, he had been tuning out the rein aids because they had become too strong. His rider had gradually increased the strength of the rein aids with him until he was running through quite a bit of pressure—he was *resisting the insistence.* A horse with a *hard mouth* is a resistant horse, and the key is to figure out what is he resisting? By keeping the primary aid polite (the rein pressure) and using a secondary aid (the wall) to cause him to stop, the gelding learned to listen and respond to the primary aid. Most horses are willing to respond to aids that have *meaning*, so we need to be thinking in terms of getting the horse to understand the aids vs. using the aids strongly in attempt to force his compliance. The aids either cause a mental understanding or they elicit a *biomechanical response*,[8] but they should not be used to forcefully manipulate the horse's body.

Balance vs. Counter Balance

Essentially a horse is either doing what we want him to do, or he isn't. When he isn't, there are two ways we can approach the situation:

1. Ride him *as if* he's doing what we want even when he isn't. In this manner we give him a guideline, or a leadership, he can conform to. This approach differs from directly addressing those things he's doing that we don't want him to do because it means we stay focused on what we do want. For example, say we want a horse to bend and turn to the right, but he's leaning to the right (so he's *falling into* the turn) rather than standing upright and *bending through* the turn. If a horse is leaning to the right it's a common tendency for the rider to feel he should lean to the left, or counter-balance him, but counter-balancing will only commit the horse to leaning. If a horse is leaning one way and the rider leans the other, then the horse has to stay leaning in order to counter-balance the rider! It's sort of like a tug of war with a rope where if one person lets go, the other will fall down. So neither horse nor rider is upright and laterally balanced because they are both committed to counter-balancing each other.

   The solution lies in the rider feeling how he would be sitting *if* the horse were upright, laterally balanced, and bending through the turn. And *if* the horse were truly bending, the rider would be sitting upright himself (not collapsing on either side of his ribcage), his pelvis would be parallel to the horse's hips, and his shoulders would parallel the horse's shoulders. So that's the way the rider

needs to sit even if the horse is leaning or tilting. The rider wants the horse to find a place of upright balance, and he will not be able to do that if the rider is counterbalancing him because that puts the rider off-center as well. So by riding the horse *as if* he's turning and bending correctly, the rider allows the horse to find his own balance and bend underneath the rider's position.

2. If the first approach doesn't work (perhaps the horse isn't able to conform to the rider), the second approach is to support whatever the horse *is* doing. Harmony means horse and rider are working in unison, yet many people think harmony means the horse is always the one to conform to the human, though sometimes the human needs to conform to the horse in order to create harmony. Once we harmonize with the horse's motion, even if it isn't what we want, we can then begin to change his movement *from the inside*. We can use the harmony we have established with the horse to change his way of going. Using the same example of turning and bending, say the horse is falling to the right and we want him to bend to the right. Bend is more about release or stretch on the outside of the body than it is about contraction on the inside, so if the horse is not bending to the right, then he's tight on the left side of his body. We want him to let go of the contraction on his left side, but if we focus on trying to force him to bend to the right he'll likely only resist by tightening more on the left.

In that case, we can support him, or harmonize with him, by riding him in a counter-bend—i.e. ask him to bend to the left (which supports his contraction on the left) while he's traveling to the right. I've done this many times with many different horses and it works amazingly well. Sometimes it takes a while for the horse to release, but when they do they are then able to bend the other way, and do so softly with no resistance.

This approach might seem counter-intuitive, but it has physiological validity. I believe the release response is in part mental as well as physical, but the body itself will more readily release tension when it is not being forced to do so. We need to encourage and allow the horse's body to release the tension so the horse can then bend the other way, and by accepting or supporting his tension on the left, we allow him to let it go.

Anytime we resist or prevent what a horse is doing we disharmonize ourselves from him. If we want him to go forward and he doesn't so we lean forward, we are no longer in balance or harmony. If we want him to bend right and he doesn't so we lean right, we are no longer in balance or harmony. If he's leaning right and we lean left to counter-balance him, we are no longer in harmony. If he's going too fast and we pull backwards on the reins, we are no longer in harmony. Our influence is just that, i.e. *influence*, meaning it is not absolute. But our influence will be considerably greater if it is exerted within a state of harmony. Harmony occurs when we ride the horse's rhythm, whatever it is. So when things aren't going well, it is better to first establish harmony before trying to exert influence. And if that means we need to *go where the horse is* to establish harmony, then so be it.

However, having said that, there is another tactic that can be effective and it's good to make a distinction between the two. It is possible to accept what a horse is doing and still ask him to do the opposite. When horses do not comply with our requests it is usually out of either fear, pain, confusion or agenda. The latter refers to the horse who is not afraid, anxious, confused, or uncomfortable but rather just not paying attention or preferring to mentally engage in something else. In that case, if I'm riding a horse and he's looking off to the right at some horses in the distance, I might ask him to make a turn to the left; if he takes off without a request, I might ask him to stop and back up; if he speeds up on straight lines, I might ask him to turn or circle, etc. So it's possible to ask a horse to do things that counter what he's doing yet still be in harmony with him while he's doing them. The difference lies in the rider's underlying intent. Anytime our thought is *"No, don't do that"* we have sacrificed harmony with what he is offering. But we can ask him to do the opposite of what he is doing while at the same time not resisting what he *is* doing. We can accept what he is offering but then ask for the opposite as if we just changed our mind and wanted to do something else instead. It can be a fine line, but the gauge is the feeling of resistance and non-acceptance within the human vs. a feeling of acceptance and allowance, and that has nothing to do with the horse per se—that feeling resides within the human.

We want to remain in harmony with a horse's body and movement even when we are asking him to make a change, and the difference feels to me like one of being *inside* the movement vs. trying to make changes from the *outside*. It's always up to the rider to create harmony. A good rider will show a horse, over the course of time, how to harmonize with the rider on his back, but ultimately the rider must initiate the harmony.

We want to ride the horse as if he's doing everything we want him to do, even when he isn't—especially when he isn't..

I try to stay connected to what he is doing while I keep my focus on what I want him to do. That approach is quite different from resisting what he is doing because I want him to do something else. The former uses the present moment as a *bridge* to connect what is happening with what I want to happen, while the latter is a non-acceptance of what is happening while trying to change it through opposition.

Resistance and Evasion

Any time a request is made of a horse he responds to it in one of three ways:
1. Resistance
2. Evasion
3. Compliance

Resistance is obvious—the horse feels stiff or braced as he refuses the request. The resistant horse pushes against the bit, and/or he tightens his back, and/or he stiffens laterally and won't bend, and/or he plants his feet and won't move at all, etc., though he does those things in varying degrees depending on the degree of resistance. Resistance is most obviously felt in the jaw and poll through the reins. The first thing a resistant horse will do is clamp or tighten his jaw and tighten or retract his poll muscles resulting in a hard and unyielding feeling in the rider's hands. The resistant horse is often referred to as having a *hard mouth*, but it is not a lack of feeling in his mouth per se. It's a protective, defensive maneuver, and unfortunately it often causes the rider to become more heavy-handed or use a stronger bit or device (such as draw reins, martingale, etc.) in attempt to eliminate the resistance. In a similar manner, many horses will tighten their belly muscles in response to harsh leg or spur aids. When they tighten or tense up they are not fluid on their feet; in fact, they will tend to want to plant or stab their feet into the ground which often leads to the rider kicking or spurring even harder.

The solution is not to try to *break through* a resistance with stronger aids, rather we want to encourage the horse to release his resistance. The first step is to give him no reason to be resistant to the request in the first place. Many times horses are resistant because requests are demanded rather than asked. I think of those cases as the horse *resisting the insistence* rather than the particular thing being insisted upon. Other common causes of resistance are fear, pain, confusion, anxiety, frustration, resentment, distraction, etc. Often times if a horse responds with resistance and the rider lightens the aid and presents the horse with a *softer feel*, the horse will respond more willingly.

One example of resistance due to pain involves a study done by the Myler brothers on horses' mouths and how they respond to different bits. The study showed that increased tongue pressure causes a resistant reaction in the horse, and physically affects his ability to move athletically by interfering with his hyoid apparatus, which is connected to the back of the tongue and plays a key role in a horse's posture. If the tongue is compressed so the hyoid apparatus is not able to function optimally a horse is mechanically unable to come onto the bit. A horse will react to increased tongue pressure in a number of ways:

1. He'll pull his tongue up in his mouth, which can interfere with his breathing.
2. He'll put his tongue over the bit which causes his tender bars to suffer the pressure.
3. He will drop back behind the bit to escape the pain (evasion), or he'll push harder against to bit in attempt to get the pressure off his tongue (resistance).
4. He'll gape his mouth open, provided it is not clamped shut with a tight noseband.

In these cases, the pain and/or restriction of the bit is causing resistance, yet many riders will apply even more pressure to the bit when they feel their horses brace, thereby continuing the cycle of resistance. The only way out of resistance through increased pressure is for the horse to learn to evade the bit by pulling back behind it. But neither resistance or evasion is compliance.

This information led to the development of the Myler bits which are designed to be more comfortable in a horse's mouth, affording him proper tongue relief, so as to not trigger the resistance caused by pain. It is most productive to think of the bit as a means of communication thereby creating compliance through cooperation and effective dialogue, and yet some riders think the purpose of a bit is to cause enough pain that the horse tries to avoid it. That reasoning is counter-productive. For one thing, pain often causes evasion rather than true compliance, but evasion *feels soft* so it is often confused with compliance. Over flexing in the neck and bringing the face behind the vertical is considered to be *behind the bit*, and it is an evasion, despite the fact that many riders think it is the way they want their horses to respond to any bit pressure.

I think it is important to make a distinction here: There is a difference between a horse *seeking a release* and *avoiding pressure*. The horse who seeks a release is an interactive partner in his own training. He has been shown that there is a right answer to every question his rider/handler poses, and he has learned that he will be rewarded when he finds that right answer. The reward will be the cessation of the aid (negative reinforcement) hopefully coupled with praise (positive reinforcement). When his *right answers* are continually rewarded, he becomes trusting, confident and actually begins to seek out the right answer. That horse is seeking a release and he is truly learning his lessons in the process. That horse also carries no negative tension in his body.

Avoiding pressure is a different scenario. If pressure is applied and it causes pain, the horse will be motivated to avoid the pain. If the pain is in his mouth, he can learn to avoid it by over-bending his neck, or gaping his mouth open, etc., but he doesn't learn the interactive reward system of voluntarily finding the right answer—he only learns to avoid pain through evasion. The problem with this type of reaction is that it feels soft to the rider, and the rider can mistake it for compliance. Not all soft feels are good—some are simply evasions. Over-flexion or bending of the neck has also become something desired by many riders in many disciplines. It has become a goal and yet it does not take into account a horse's *biomechanical integrity*. [9] Over-flexion causes the horse to become *disconnected* in his neck—i.e. his neck no longer operates in unity with the rest of his body, and as a result there is no *connection* through is back from his mouth to his hind feet. The resistant horse is obviously tense, but the evasive horse is tense as well, he has just learned to become hyper-mobile in the wrong parts of his body—often in the middle of his neck (aka a rubber neck).

A defining difference lies in whether or not the horse has released the tension in his jaw and poll. A horse can over flex his neck (at the third to fourth cervical vertebrae) and his poll can appear flexed as well, but the feeling in his jaw and poll is hard—sometimes they feel set as if in concrete. We want to be able to laterally flex the poll and to have the horse willingly turn his head left or right with a feeling of relaxation specifically at the poll. He will need to release any tension in his jaw in order to do this, and a mobile jaw often results in a soft chewing/swallowing motion of the mouth. Tight or restrictive nosebands interfere with the good motions of the mouth, and if a horse needs a tight noseband to keep his mouth shut I would guarantee there is tension in his jaw and poll. The mobilization of the jaw and the lateral release of the poll are the *gateway* to access the rest of the horse's body. They are also the first place of defense, so in response to any tension or anxiety a horse feels he will first tighten his jaw and poll. Becoming hyper-mobile in the middle of his neck does nothing to ease the tension in his jaw/poll even though it results in the look of flexion and a soft feeling in the rider's hands. Faulty flexion or over flexion breaks the connection from the mouth to the hind feet. It is very common in horse training today in all disciplines, yet it is an undeserved assault on a horse's mental and mechanical integrity.

I remember the first time I felt the connection between the mouth and the hind feet. I was riding a Hannoverian horse I had bred and raised, and while I knew conceptually what I wanted I wasn't sure what it felt like or exactly how to achieve it. I persisted in using the traditional methods—rhythm, bend, lateral work, etc.—but this horse had a tendency to be heavy in the hand. I don't recall exactly what I did, but I do remember that suddenly his entire body took on a different feeling. He felt light, round and springy on his feet, and when I asked him to stop it was as if he literally stepped his hind feet into my hands. I merely closed my fingers on the reins and I felt his hind feet stop. I have ridden many horses who would stop obediently to a light request, but this was different. I could feel the connection through his whole body. It was as if he was stepping into my hands and the feeling was soft but also *alive*. It was a light bulb moment. If we can experience things like this even once then we at least know they are possible—and if they are possible, they can be replicated. One success can cause a chain reaction.

Persistence vs. Insistence

It is helpful to distinguish between persistence and insistence when making requests of a horse. Some people think if they don't insist on what they want it means they are relinquishing their authority, but that is a human perception and not the way the horse sees it. Control is a huge issue with many people. We often feel a compelling urge to control the people and events in our lives, including our horses. Yet control has an unyielding feel to it, a feel that many horses will automatically react to adversely. Too often the feel of insistence from the human is met with opposition in the horse, and too often the human's insistence becomes increasingly stronger and/or more painful as a result.

Persistence, on the other hand, has a different feel to it. For one thing, we don't need to increase the pressure or strength of our request to persist. Persistence is about waiting. It is about accepting *what is*, making a request for a change, and then waiting for the change to happen. We don't give up our request when we persist, but there is not the rigid feel to it that there is with insistence. And yet that more subtle feeling of persistence can sometimes make us feel as if we are not in control or we are lacking authority. Control has an absolute quality to it. We are either in control or not, and if we feel we are not then we will get stronger and more insistent to try to maintain a sense of control. When we relinquish that edge that control carries with it, it sometimes feels as if we are relinquishing the control as well, but we aren't.

Ironically, we often have more influence over a horse when we give up our notion of controlling him.

The reason for that lies in the predator/prey conflict. Our need to control causes us to act in a predatory manner. To us, control means restraint, and restraint to a prey animal is predatory.

We need to look at the underlying issue behind control. We feel a compelling urge to control things—people, animals, situations, etc.—because we want to feel better inside. We want to feel calm vs. afraid, or we want to feel confident vs. insecure, or we want to feel accomplished vs. inadequate, or we want to feel happy vs. sad, etc., and we think if we can just control that *something* outside ourselves that is causing us to feel badly, then we will feel good inside. And in that sense control is ultimately about self. The only thing we can control in life is ourselves. We need to find that good feeling we want from the inside and let that feeling emanate outward vs. trying to control everything outside ourselves in the hope that will change how we feel on the inside. So very often when we feel the urge to control that causes us to become insistent or demanding with our horses, that need is coming from our own inability to control our inner state of being and really has nothing to do with the horse. The horse is merely a mirror of what is lacking within ourselves. We make it about him, but ultimately it is not.

Insistence arises from a lack of inner composure, a lack of inner control, and a lack in the belief that we will be able to elicit a change. Persistence arises from an inner place of being okay with whatever is happening in the moment coupled with the knowledge that it can and will change. If we feel empowered in our ability to make a change, then we will be able to wait for that change; we will be able to simply persist, or stay with the request until the change happens. But if we doubt our ability to make a change then we often resort to insisting the change occur. Insistence often arises from self-doubt and insecurity, and many horses suffer due to human insecurity. In discussing this topic with riders I have had many of them say *"But there are times when I have to know that my horse will do what I tell him to do."* I suggest they consider an example of driving a car. What if someone told you they could NOT have a car wreck—it was simply not an option for them. If someone told me that I would tell them they ought to never get into a car! There are no guarantees in life, but that doesn't mean we can't be prudent and increase our chances for success. And the best way to do that is to stay focused on the proactive things we can do to insure success vs. focusing on all the things that we don't want to happen, and then trying to prevent them from happening.

The Wind Sock

When a horse is out of control he will usually stiffen his body as his hind legs actively attempt to send him into flight. I liken his tense body to a wind sock which is made of nylon. Let's say the wind is blowing at 10 mph and that amount of wind does not fill up the sock, but rather causes it to flap about limply. Then the wind picks up and is blowing at 30 mph, which not only completely fills the wind sock but causes it to whip about wildly. The optimal amount of wind, the amount that fills the sock so it maintains a consistent shape but does not cause it to whip about, is 20 mph. We can compare the horse's body to the wind sock, and the wind is his energy. If his hind legs are lackluster he will go along lazily with no integrity to his movement, rather like the limp wind sock in a 10 mph wind. If his hind legs produce just the right amount of energy (i.e. his optimal tempo) his movement will be energetic yet controllable—his wind sock is full but not wildly whipping. If his hind legs produce too much energy, like when he is frightened and wants to get away, his body will be too full of energy and he will become out of control, like the wind sock in a 30 mph wind. There is no way for the wind sock to accept more than a 20 mph wind without whipping wildly as long as it is made of nylon, just as the horse's body is not able to accept more than optimal energy without becoming uncontrollable. The only way for the wind sock to accept more wind would be if it were made of elastic, then a wind stronger than 20 mph would cause it to expand rather than whip about.

The horse becomes out of control because his body is filled with too much energy and there is no expansion. In fact, his survival depends on his feet propelling a tight body, not a limp one, so there is a natural tendency for his body to become tight like the nylon wind sock. However, it would be to our advantage as riders if his body were made of elastic so extra energy would cause it to expand rather than fly out of control. Expansion in his body would be useful at those times when something frightens him as a means to keep him from exploding, but expansion is also a way to give his movement maximum expression. A horse who proudly fills himself up with containable energy is an impressive sight. We see this type of action often in stallions putting on a show for mares. So elasticizing the body has a safety value as well as a performance value. The question is how do we begin to elasticize his body, and the answer is through lateral steps and bend.

Lateral steps are simply sideways steps, such as:

- The front feet moving around the haunches (a turn on the haunches,
- The hind feet moving around the front feet (a turn on the forehand)
- Both front and hind feet moving forward and sideways (a leg yield)
- Both front and hind feet moving sideways only (a side pass)
- Front feet moving one way as the hind feet move the other, causing the horse to turn from the center as if spinning a coke bottle (a turn on the epi-center)

Lateral steps in both directions and in both front and hind feet are a good beginning toward elasticizing the horse's body.

Bend means the horse's spine (from poll to tail) conforms to a curved line. Bend does not occur with absolute evenness throughout the spine, and all bend is accompanied by axial rotation between certain vertebrae (a swivel like motion similar to turning a door knob which causes the ribcage to rotate in the bend), but the horse can exhibit the appearance of an even bend through his body. If a horse leans into a turn, his ribcage is rotated so his withers come to the inside. That's what causes him to lean or fall to the inside. If the horse bends through a turn his ribcage rotates so his withers go to the outside.

Bend is not about contraction on the inside of the body, but rather expansion or lengthening on the outside.

Bend to the left begins to elasticize or expand the right side of his body, and vice versa. Adding lateral steps to bend is particularly beneficial.

One good exercise is to walk the horse around a small circle, as if walking around a tree trunk. Get a nice bend and even fluid footfalls coupled with a feeling of relaxation. I find it helpful for many riders to count the rhythm either in their head or out loud. Since the walk is a 4 beat gait, you can count *one-two-three-four/one-two-three-four...etc.* to keep the rhythm active and symmetrical. Then begin to enlarge the circle by increasing the bend outward as the horse's feet also step outward—so going to the left he would be in a left bend while the right side of his body is expanding outward and his feet are stepping toward the right. When he can enlarge the circle equally well both directions he is on his way to becoming expandable in his body. Another variation is to ask the hind feet to travel a little bigger circle than the front feet as he moves around the imaginary tree trunk. If something frightens him causing his energy to increase, his expandable body has the capacity to absorb that energy rather than causing him to tighten and simply try to take off. The rider needs to become adept at gaining a good bend and/or lateral steps because when the horse's energy increases the rider's efforts will need to be on maintaining the bend and/or lateral movement rather than opposing the horse's desire to flee. Both bend and lateral steps are not things a horse naturally does in flight mode, so they become a good way to take him mentally and physically out of flight mode and return him to the influence of the rider.

In the Middle

Due to the way a horse's eyesight is structured, his vision is designed so he can use each eyeball separately—one to scan the left side of his body, and the other his right side—when his head is down as he's grazing. He has a blind spot right in front of and behind him, which further augments his sense of a divided world. I believe a horse naturally processes his world as two halves rather than one whole, though if one eye catches sight of something suspicious he will raise his head and focus both eyes on it. Even when he has both eyes on it, he will look to the right and back to the object, then to the left and back to the object trying to integrate the two halves and see the whole picture. The relevance of this to our riding is that when we sit on his back we are sitting *in the middle*. The middle refers to the center of left and right and not necessarily of front to back. The middle refers to the alignment of his spine which runs down the middle of his back, so we sit in the center of his body.

Our influence and the feeling of our position for him is in the middle where he doesn't intuitively think. Part of the challenge of our training is to first get him to accept our influence from the middle. We begin that by directing his attention and his feet left or right at our discretion, but even when we get him thinking and turning both directions readily we need to carry that to the next level, which is to get him aligning his thoughts and body under us—i.e. in the middle.

There is an old expression that describes a horse as *being on the seat*, which refers to a horse who will attempt to remain aligned and balanced under the rider's seat and take his direction from that point of contact. In order to turn his body over to his rider in that manner he must first be willing and able to find the rider's influence in the middle. He must be able to think from the center and not from either left or right, although the latter is his natural tendency. It is important that we sit centered over his back and equally weighted on each side. That doesn't preclude the giving of weight aids, but unless we are actively giving a weight aid our default position should be equally weighted. Our upper body and seat should remain centered, as our hands and legs bring the horse's awareness to that place under our seat which is in the middle. In that sense, we *ride both sides toward the middle*. However, that does not mean we use the reins to pull the head or neck back, down or inward. It means we bring the horse's *awareness* down the middle as we send his hind legs forward under our seat.

The first challenge for aligning the horse in the middle is to find the same alignment within our own body. I have yet to see a rider who naturally sits symmetrically. The degree of our own asymmetry varies from slight to great, but we are all crooked to some extent. Rider position is my pet project, but it is beyond the scope of the written word to address. Most riders need instant feedback because their asymmetrical habits are so ingrained. Suffice it to say, a visual image I use is one of what I call the *clicked on cowboy*. When I was young we had plastic horses and cowboy riders we could put on them. The riders were perfectly symmetrical and had bowed legs so if you pushed them down they clicked onto the horse's back. The *clicked on cowboys* did not have one heel drawn up, or one arm pulled back, or one side of their ribcage collapsed, or their head tilted, or their hips off center over the horse's back, etc. When they clicked on to the horse they were even, symmetrical, centered, and balanced. If only that were so easy for us!

There is nothing in a horse's natural state that requires him to have a keen sense of the middle—rather his eyesight is designed for thinking left or right, so developing the sense of a middle ground is a unique aspect of being ridden by a human being. It also means he needs to be secure and trusting enough to *turn himself over* to his rider for in his mind, if he is paying attention to the rider in the middle then who is looking out for danger on the left or the right? Many riders think horses are being stubborn when they don't pay attention to the rider, but it takes careful work to build enough trust and confidence in a horse for him to put his safety literally in human hands. We take it for granted that a horse isn't going to be pursued by a predator

Of Life and Horses

when we ride him, but he doesn't know that. Wariness is inherent to his being and his survival as a species. Showing him how to operate from direction in the middle of his two worlds (the left and the right) is another way we take him out of his instinctive survival mode, but he must feel trust and confidence in our leadership to give himself over like that.

Summary

I have found the vast majority of horses want to get along, and while there are some who seem to be disagreeable they are likely confused, frightened or they have learned to be defensive around humans. I think we would do well to give any horse the benefit of the doubt. That doesn't mean we don't address whatever their issue is, but rather we don't too quickly label them as defiant or stubborn or mean or stupid or whatever. We should first look to ourselves and try to determine how the horse sees us. Horses didn't choose to be confined and used for our pleasure. They didn't ask to be kept in ways that defy their nature. They don't care about the ways in which they can boost our egos, and yet in the majority of cases they do their best to make the most of what life has thrown them. We should be grateful for that if nothing else, and show some appreciation. If we can learn to effectively communicate and set our emotions and egos aside, our interactions will be calmer and more productive. Horses are just as stressed by their uncontrollable behaviors as we are. They don't want to be like that, but punishment of the behaviors is not the answer. We need to learn to elicit their cooperation through effective communication.

Endnotes

1. There are a number of books on clicker training, and one I recommend is *Getting to Yes: Clicker Training for Improved Horsemanship* by Sharon Foley.
2. I was unable to find a direct source for this quote, but it is associated with martial arts and/or The Tao.
3. Commonly attributed to President Theodore Roosevelt, but it originated from an African proverb.
4. There is a chapter in my first book—*Of Life and Horses—The Nature of the Horse*—that explains the primitive vs. the thinking brain and how they affect training.
5. This is a term I heard often as a kid, but I run into horse owners today who aren't familiar with it. Basically it refers to a horse who is extremely reluctant to go forward—so much so that he can plant his feet and refuse to move. If pressured to move in this state the horse may rear. I use this term later on as well.
6. This label is explained in my first book *Of Life and Horses: The Nature of the Horse*. It refers to a horse who is afraid, but hunkers down like the rabbit hiding from the nearby dog—i.e. he internalizes his fear. If the dog goes away, nothing happens. But if the dog gets too close, the rabbit suddenly explodes up out of the grass and takes off. Some horses can be standing still seemingly quiet and then suddenly explode, like the hunkered down rabbit.
7. It's easier to visualize a *turn on the forehand* or a *turn on the haunches* if you substitute the word *around* for *on*. So a turn *on* the forehand is actually a turn *around* the forehand, which means the hind feet are the ones moving. In a turn on the haunches the front feet are moving *around* the haunches.

8   A biomechanical response (or impulse) is one in which something we do naturally triggers the response. The most effective aids we have for influencing equine movement are our weight aids. They often trigger a natural mechanical response in the horse, though it may or may not be the response we desire. This is a compelling reason why it's important for riders to learn to sit square, centered and balanced so our weight aids can be easily distinguished by the horse.

9   Any living body operates in a mechanical manner. It's called biomechanical because it refers to the mechanics of a *bio* or living being. Biomechanical integrity refers to the ways in which the equine body was designed to operate within mechanical parameters.

About the Author

Ann Bradley attended Kansas State University and her love for horses goes back more than fifty years to her childhood. From the Mission Valley Pony Club to working on a Wyoming cattle ranch, she showed hunter/jumper, broke and started colts, galloped and conditioned racehorses, and was the hunt seat instructor for the Park College Equine Program. Ms. Bradley is currently a freelance trainer and riding instructor in the Kansas City area.

Photo of the author taken circa 1974

Made in the USA
San Bernardino, CA
06 July 2013